# BUDDHISM
# WITHOUT
# BELIEFS

# BUDDHISM WITHOUT BELIEFS

*A Contemporary Guide to Awakening*

STEPHEN BATCHELOR

BLOOMSBURY

Some of the material in chapters 'Rebirth' and 'Imagination'
has appeared in *Tricycle: The Buddhist Review*.

First published in the USA 1997 by Riverhead Books
a division of G. P. Putnam's Sons

First published in Great Britain 1997
This paperback edition first published 1998
Bloomsbury Publishing Plc, 38 Soho Square,
London W1V 5DF

A CIP catalogue record for this book is available
from the British Library

ISBN 0 7475 3843 3

10  9

Printed in Great Britain by Clays Ltd, St Ives plc

*In memory of*
*Osbert Moore (Ñāṇamoli Thera) 1905–1960*
*and Harold Musson (Ñāṇavīra Thera) 1920–1965*

# CONTENTS

*Emperor Wu of Liang asked the great master Bodhidharma, "What is the highest meaning of the holy truths?" Bodhidharma said, "Empty, without holiness." The emperor said, "Who is facing me?" Bodhidharma replied, "I don't know."*

—*The Blue Cliff Record*

*We do not receive wisdom, we must discover it for ourselves, after a journey through the wilderness, which no one else can make for us, which no one can spare us, for our wisdom is the point of view from which we come at last to regard the world.*

—Marcel Proust

# PREFACE

I HAVE TRIED to write a book on Buddhism in ordinary English that avoids the use of foreign words, technical terms, lists, and jargon. The one exception is the term "dharma," for which I can find no English equivalent.

Broadly speaking, "dharma" refers to the teachings of the Buddha as well as to those aspects of reality and experience with which his teachings are concerned. "Dharma practice" refers to the way of life undertaken by someone who is inspired by such teachings.

I am grateful to Helen Tworkov and Lorraine Kisly, who persuaded me to write this book, and for Lorraine's editorial guidance, which kept the aim of the task in focus and reined in my tendency to digress. I am likewise grateful to Mary South of Riverhead for her final editing of the manuscript. Thanks also to the Sharpham Trust, Devon, England, and the Buddhist Retreat Centre, Ixopo, South Africa, which provided beautiful rural settings in which to work on the text; and to my wife, Martine, who supplied unwavering support throughout.

Stephen Batchelor
Sharpham College
September 1996

# GROUND

*Do not be satisfied with hearsay or with tradition or with legendary lore or with what has come down in scriptures or with conjecture or with logical inference or with weighing evidence or with liking for a view after pondering over it or with someone else's ability or with the thought "The monk is our teacher." When you know in yourselves: "These things are wholesome, blameless, commended by the wise, and being adopted and put into effect they lead to welfare and happiness," then you should practice and abide in them. . .*

— The Buddha

*Kalama Sutta*

# AWAKENING

*As long as my vision was not fully clear . . . regarding four ennobling truths, I did not claim to have realized authentic awakening. . . .*

—The Buddha

L ET'S GO BACK to the beginning: to the awakening of Siddhartha Gautama, aka the Tathagata, Shakyamuni, the World Honored One—the Buddha himself. He was the one who set the wheel of dharma spinning in the first place. He was the one who pointed out the central path (the famous "Middle Way"). He was the trailblazer. His are the footprints we will find at the end of the track.

Let's start with the Buddha's first discourse, delivered to his five former ascetic companions in the Deer Park at Sarnath, near Benares. It was here, several weeks after the awakening and his ensuing ambivalence about saying anything at all, that compassion moved him to embrace the anguish of others. Plunging into the treacherous sea of words, he "set in motion the wheel of the dharma."

This short discourse can be summed up as follows: The Buddha declares how he has found the central path through avoiding indulgence and mortification. He then describes four ennobling truths: those of anguish, its origins, its cessation, and the path leading to its cessation. Anguish, he says, is to be understood, its origins to be let go of, its cessation to be realized, and the path to be cultivated. And this is precisely what he himself has done: he has understood anguish, let go of its origins, realized its cessation, and cultivated the path. Only through knowing these truths, knowing how to act upon them, and knowing that he has acted upon them can he claim to have found "authentic awakening."

DESPITE THE BUDDHA'S own succinct account of his awakening, it has come to be represented (even by Buddhists) as something quite different. Awakening has become a mystical experience, a moment of transcendent revelation of the Truth. Religious interpretations invariably reduce complexity to uniformity while elevating matter-of-factness to holiness. Over time, increasing emphasis has been placed on a single Absolute Truth, such as "the Deathless," "the Unconditioned," "the Void," "Nirvana," "Buddha Nature," etc., rather than on an interwoven complex of truths.

And the crucial distinction that *each truth requires being acted upon in its own particular way* (*understanding* anguish, *letting go of* its origins, *realizing* its cessation, and *cultivating* the path) has been relegated to the margins of specialist doctrinal knowledge. Few Buddhists today are probably even aware of the distinction.

Yet in failing to make this distinction, four ennobling truths to be acted upon are neatly turned into four propositions of fact to be believed. The first truth becomes: "Life Is Suffering"; the second: "The Cause of Suffering Is Craving"—and so on. At precisely this juncture, Buddhism becomes a religion. A Buddhist is someone who *believes* these four propositions. In leveling out these truths into propositions that claim to be true, Buddhists are distinguished from Christians, Muslims, and Hindus, who believe different sets of propositions. The four ennobling truths become principal dogmas of the belief system known as "Buddhism."

The Buddha was not a mystic. His awakening was not a shattering insight into a transcendent Truth that revealed to him the mysteries of God. He did not claim to have had an experience that granted him privileged, esoteric knowledge of how the universe ticks. Only as Buddhism became more and more of a religion were such grandiose claims imputed to his awakening. In describing to the five ascetics what his awakening meant, he spoke of having discovered complete freedom of heart and mind from the compulsions of craving. He called such freedom the taste of the dharma.

THE BUDDHA AWOKE from the sleep of existential confusion. So shocking and unexpected was this experience that he initially assumed that were he to speak of it no one would understand him. A person who is asleep is either lost in deep unconsciousness or absorbed in a dream. Metaphorically, this was how the Buddha must have seen both his previous self as well as everyone else he had known: they either were blind to the questions of existence or sought consolation from them in metaphysical or religious fantasies. His awakening, however, brought *both* the questions *and* their resolutions into vivid and unanticipated focus.

The Buddha woke up to the nature of the human dilemma and a way to its resolution. The first two truths (anguish and its origins) describe the dilemma, the second two (cessation and the path) its resolution. He awoke to a set of interrelated truths rooted in the immediacy of experience here and now.

The Buddha experienced these truths as ennobling. Awakening was not just the acquisition of a more enlightened viewpoint. It granted a natural integrity, dignity, and authority to his life. Although the five ascetics had vowed not to acknowledge their apostate former companion, as he entered the Deer Park in Sarnath and came toward them, they found themselves standing up to offer him respect. In spite of themselves, they were unable to resist the authority of Gautama's presence.

❧

AN UNAWAKENED EXISTENCE, in which we drift unaware on a surge of habitual impulses, is both ignoble and undignified. Instead of a natural and noncoercive authority, we impose our will on others either through manipulation and intimidation or by appealing to the opinions of those more powerful than ourselves. Authority becomes a question of force rather than of integrity.

Instead of presenting himself as a savior, the Buddha saw himself as a healer. He presented his truths in the form of a medical diagnosis, prognosis, and treatment. If you have a pain in your chest, you first need to acknowledge it. Then you will go to a doctor for an examination. His diagnosis will both identify the cause of pain and tell you if it is curable. If it is curable, he will advise you to follow a course of treatment. Likewise, the Buddha acknowledged the existential condition of anguish. On examination he found its origins to lie in self-centered craving. He realized that this could cease, and prescribed the cultivation of a path of life embracing all aspects of human experience as an effective treatment.

WHILE "BUDDHISM" SUGGESTS another belief system, "dharma practice" suggests a course of action. The four ennobling truths are not propositions to believe; they are challenges to act.

There is a passage in *Alice's Adventures in Wonderland* in which Alice enters a room to find a bottle marked with the label "Drink Me." The label does not tell Alice what is inside the bottle but tells her what to do with it. When the Buddha presented his four truths, he first described what each referred to, then enjoined his listeners to act upon them. Once we grasp what he refers to by "anguish," we are enjoined to *understand* it—as though it bore the label "Understand Me." The truth of anguish becomes an injunction to act.

The first truth challenges our habitual relationship to anguish. In the broadest sense, it challenges how we relate to our existence as such: our birth, sickness, aging, and death. To what extent do we fail to understand these realities and their implications? How much time is spent in distraction or oblivion? When we are gripped by a worry, for example, what do we do? We might struggle to shake it off. Or we try to convince ourselves that things are not the way they seem, failing which we seek to preoccupy ourselves with something else. How often do we embrace that worry, accept our situation, and try to understand it?

Anguish maintains its power only as long as we allow it to intimidate us. By habitually regarding it as fearful and threatening, we fail to see the words etched on it by the Buddha: "Understand Me." If we try to avoid a powerful wave looming above us on the beach, it will send us crashing

7

into the sand and surf. But if we face it head-on and dive right into it, we discover only water.

To understand a worry is to know it calmly and clearly for what it is: transient, contingent, and devoid of intrinsic identity. Whereas to misunderstand it is to freeze it into something fixed, separate, and independent. Worrying about whether a friend still likes us, for example, becomes an isolated thing rather than part of a process emerging from a stream of contingencies. This perception induces in turn a mood of feeling psychologically blocked, stuck, obsessed. The longer this undignified state persists, the more we become incapable of action. The challenge of the first truth is to act before habitual reactions incapacitate us.

A SIMILAR PROCEDURE can be applied to the other truths. Just as the presence of anguish is an opportunity for understanding, so the presence of the self-centered craving that underlies it is an opportunity for letting go. Such craving is manifest in a variety of ways: it extends from simple egoism and selfishness to that deep-seated, anxious longing for security to fear of rejection by those we love to the compulsion to have a cigarette. Whenever such feelings arise, the habitual reaction is either to indulge them or to deny them. Which again blinds us to the phrase stamped on them by the Buddha: "Let Go!"

"Letting go" is not a euphemism for stamping out craving by other means. As with anguish, letting go begins with understanding: a calm and clear acceptance of what is happening. While craving (the second truth) may be the origin or cause of anguish (the first truth), this does not mean they are two separate things—any more than the sprout is separate from the daffodil that emerges from it. Just as craving crystallizes into anguish, so does understanding flower into letting go.

Letting go of a craving is not rejecting it but allowing it to be itself: a contingent state of mind that once arisen will pass away. Instead of forcibly freeing ourselves from it, notice how its very nature is to free itself. To let it go is like releasing a snake that you have been clutching in your hand. By identifying with a craving ("*I* want this," "*I* don't want that"), you tighten the clutch and intensify its resistance. Instead of being a state of mind that you have, it becomes a compulsion that has you. As with understanding anguish, the challenge in letting go of craving is to act before habitual reactions incapacitate us.

By letting go of craving it will finally cease. This cessation allows us to realize, if only momentarily, the freedom, openness, and ease of the central path. This sudden gap in the rush of self-centered compulsion and fear allows us to see with unambiguous immediacy and clarity the transient, unreliable, and contingent nature of reality. Dharma practice at this moment has relinquished the last traces of belief; it is founded on authentic vision born from experience. It no longer requires the support of moralistic rules and religious ritual; it is grounded in integrity and creative autonomy. In revealing life in all its vulnerability, it becomes the doorway to compassion.

IN THE CESSATION of craving, we touch that dimension of experience that is timeless: the playful, unimpeded contingency of things emerging from conditions only to become conditions for something else. This is emptiness: not a cosmic vacuum but the unborn, undying, infinitely creative dimension of life. It is known as the "womb of awakening"; it is the clearing in the still center of becoming, the track on which the centered person moves. And it whispers: "Realize Me."

But no sooner is it glimpsed than it is gone. Cessation of

craving is like a momentary gap in the clouds. The sun shines brilliantly for a few moments, only to be covered over again. We find ourselves back in the humbling fog of anguish, craving, habit, restlessness, distraction. But with a difference: now we know where this track goes. We have set foot in the territory for which these words are just a map.

We realize that until this point we have not really been on the path at all. We have been following hunches, heeding the words of those we respect, exploring blind alleys, stumbling and guessing. No matter how strong our resolve and conviction, all along there may have been a nagging unease that we didn't really know where we were going. Each step felt hesitant and forced, and we were terribly alone. The difference between then and now is like the idea of sex and the first experience of it. On the one hand, the act is a momentous and irrevocable step; on the other hand, it is just a part of life.

Henceforth, resolve to cultivate this path becomes unwavering yet entirely natural. It is simply what we do. There is no longer any sense of self-consciousness, contrivance, awkwardness, or hesitation. Awakening is no longer seen as something to attain in the distant future, for it is not a thing but a process—and this process is the path itself. But neither does this render us in any way perfect or infallible. We are quite capable of subverting this process to the interests of our far-from-extinct desires, ambitions, hatreds, jealousies, and fears. We have not been elevated to the lofty heights of awakening; awakening has been knocked off its pedestal into the turmoil and ambiguity of everyday life.

There is nothing particularly religious or spiritual about this path. It encompasses everything we do. It is an authentic way of being in the world. It begins with how we understand the kind of reality we inhabit and the kind of beings we are that inhabit such a reality. Such a vision underpins the values that inform our ideas, the choices we make, the words we utter, the deeds we perform, the work we do. It provides the ethical ground for mindful and focused awareness, which in turn further deepens our understanding of the kind of reality we inhabit and the kind of beings we are that inhabit such a reality. And so on.

To cultivate these diverse elements of our existence means to nurture them as we would a garden. Just as a garden needs to be protected, tended, and cared for, so do ethical integrity, focused awareness, and understanding. No matter how deep our insight into the empty and contingent nature of things, that alone will do little to cultivate these qualities. Each of these areas in life becomes a challenge, an injunction to act. There is no room for complacency, for they all bear a tag that declares: "Cultivate Me."

THE ACTIONS THAT accompany the four truths describe the trajectory of dharma practice: understanding anguish leads to letting go of craving, which leads to realizing its cessation, which leads to cultivating the path. These are not four separate activities but four phases within the process of awakening itself. Understanding matures into letting go; letting go culminates in realization; realization impels cultivation.

This trajectory is no linear sequence of "stages" through which we "progress." We do not leave behind an earlier stage in order to advance to the next rung of some hierarchy. All four activities are part of a single continuum of action. Dharma practice cannot be reduced to any one of them; it is configured from them all. As soon as understanding is isolated from letting go, it degrades into mere intellectuality. As soon as letting go is isolated from understanding, it declines into spiritual posturing. The fabric of dharma practice is woven from the threads of these interrelated activities, each of which is defined through its relation to the others.

THE BUDDHA'S FIRST discourse convinced the five ascetics that he was onto something. So they stayed with him,
listened to his teaching, and came to awakening themselves.
They too understood anguish, let go of craving, realized cessation, and embarked on the cultivation of the path. They too
achieved freedom of heart and mind from the compulsions of
craving. The words used to describe their awakening are the
same as those used to describe the Buddha's own. Henceforth,
at the conclusion of the Buddha's discourses, it would often be
reported not only how many people had come to awakening
through that particular teaching but to what degree.

The early discourses suggest that awakening was a common occurrence among those who listened to the Buddha
and acted upon what he said. A difference in degree was
acknowledged between those who had experienced the initial
moment of awakening and entered the path, and those who
had further cultivated the path and even reached the point
where the habit of craving was extinguished. But access to the
process of awakening itself was relatively straightforward
and did not entail any great fuss.

Yet as Buddhism became institutionalized as a religion,
awakening became progressively more inaccessible. Those
who controlled the institutions maintained that awakening
was so exalted that generally it could be attained only with
the detachment and purity of heart achieved through monas-
tic discipline. Even then, they admitted, it was rare. To
explain this state of affairs they appealed to the Indian idea of
the "degeneration of time," a notion that regards the course
of history as a process of inexorable decline. According to this
notion, those who lived at the time of the Buddha were
simply less degenerate, more "spiritual," than the corrupted
mass of humanity today.

Periodically, however, such views were challenged. The doors of awakening were thrown open to those barred from it by the strictures and dogmas of a privileged elite. Laity, women, the uneducated—the disempowered—were invited to taste the freedom of the dharma for themselves. Awakening was not a remote goal to be attained in a future lifetime. No: awakening was right here, unfolding in your own mind at this very moment.

To put it bluntly, the central question Buddhists have faced from the beginning is this: Is awakening close by or far away? Is it readily accessible or available only through supreme effort? If its proximity and ease of access are emphasized, there is the danger of trivializing it, of not according it the value and significance it deserves. Yet if its distance and difficulty of access are emphasized, there is the danger of placing it out of reach, of turning it into an icon of perfection to be worshipped from afar.

Doesn't the question itself deceive us? Aren't we tricked by its either/or logic into assuming that only one option can be true? Couldn't the ambiguous logic of both/and be more appropriate here? Awakening is indeed close by—*and* supreme effort is required to realize it. Awakening is indeed far away—*and* readily accessible.

# AGNOSTICISM

*Suppose, Malunkyaputta, a man were wounded by an arrow thickly smeared with poison, and his friends and companions brought a surgeon to treat him. The man would say: "I will not let the surgeon pull out the arrow until I know the name and clan of the man who wounded me; whether the bow that wounded me was a long bow or a crossbow; whether the arrow that wounded me was hoof-tipped or curved or barbed."*

*All this would still not be known to that man and meanwhile he would die. So too, Malunkyaputta, if anyone should say: "I will not lead the noble life under the Buddha until the Buddha declares to me whether the world is eternal or not eternal, finite or infinite; whether the soul is the same as or different from the body; whether or not an awakened one continues or ceases to exist after death," that would still remain undeclared by the Buddha and meanwhile that person would die.*

—The Buddha

IF YOU GO to Asia and visit a *wat* (Thailand) or *gompa* (Tibet), you will enter something that looks very much like an abbey, a church, or cathedral, being run by people who look like monks or priests, displaying objects that look like icons, which are enshrined in alcoves that look like chapels and revered by people who look like worshippers.

If you talk to one of the people who look like monks, you will learn that he has a view of the world that seems very much like a belief system, revealed a long time ago by someone else who is revered like a god, after whose death saintly individuals have interpreted the revelations in ways like theology. There have been schisms and reforms, and these have given rise to institutions that are just like churches.

Buddhism, it would seem, is a religion.

Or is it?

When asked what he was doing, the Buddha replied that he taught "anguish and the ending of anguish." When asked about metaphysics (the origin and end of the universe, the identity or difference of body and mind, his existence or nonexistence after death), he remained silent. He said the dharma was permeated by a single taste: freedom. He made no claims to uniqueness or divinity and did not have recourse to a term we would translate as "God."

Gautama encouraged a life that steered a middle course between indulgence and mortification. He described himself as an openhanded teacher without an esoteric doctrine reserved for an elite. Before he died he refused to appoint a successor, remarking that people should be responsible for their own freedom. Dharma practice would suffice as their guide.

This existential, therapeutic, and liberating agnosticism was articulated in the language of Gautama's place and time: the dynamic cultures of the Gangetic basin in the sixth century B.C.E. A radical critic of many deeply held views of his times, he was nonetheless a creature of those times. The axioms for living that he foresaw as lasting long after his death were refracted through the symbols, metaphors, and imagery of his world.

Religious elements, such as worship of the Buddha's person and uncritical acceptance of his teachings, were doubtless present in the first communities that formed around Gautama. Even if for five hundred years after his death his followers resisted the temptation to represent him as a quasi-divine figure, they eventually did so. As the dharma was challenged by other systems of thought in its homeland and spread abroad into foreign cultures such as China, ideas that had been part of the worldview of sixth-century-B.C.E. India became hardened into dogmas. It was not long before a self-respecting Buddhist would be expected to hold (and defend) opinions about the origin and the end of the universe, whether body and mind were identical or different, and the fate of the Buddha after death.

HISTORICALLY, BUDDHISM HAS tended to lose its agnostic dimension through becoming institutionalized as a religion (i.e., a revealed belief system valid for all time, controlled by an elite body of priests). At times this process has been challenged and even reversed (one thinks of iconoclastic Indian tantric sages, early Zen masters in China, eccentric yogins of Tibet, forest monks of Burma and Thailand). But in traditional Asian societies this never lasted long. The power of organized religion to provide sovereign states with a bulwark of moral legitimacy while simultaneously assuaging the desperate piety of the disempowered swiftly reasserted itself—usually by subsuming the rebellious ideas into the canons of a revised orthodoxy.

Consequently, as the dharma emigrates westward, it is treated as a religion—albeit an "Eastern" one. The very term "Buddhism" (an invention of Western scholars) reinforces the idea that it is a creed to be lined up alongside other creeds. Christians in particular seek to enter into dialogue with their Buddhist brethren, often as part of a broader agenda to find common ground with "those of faith" to resist the sweeping tide of Godless secularism. At interfaith gatherings, Buddhists are wheeled out to present their views on everything from nuclear weapons to the ordination of women and then scheduled to drone Tibetan chants at the evening slot for collective worship.

This transformation of Buddhism into a religion obscures and distorts the encounter of the dharma with contemporary agnostic culture. The dharma in fact might well have more in common with Godless secularism than with the bastions of religion. Agnosticism may serve as a more fertile common ground for dialogue than, for example, a tortured attempt to make Buddhist sense of Allah.

THE FORCE OF the term "agnosticism" has been lost. It has come to mean: not to hold an opinion about the questions of life and death; to say "I don't know" when you really mean "I don't want to know." When allied (and confused) with atheism, it has become part of the attitude that legitimizes an indulgent consumerism and the unreflective conformism dictated by mass media.

For T. H. Huxley, who coined the term in 1869, agnosticism was as demanding as any moral, philosophical, or religious creed. Rather than a creed, though, he saw it as a *method* realized through "the rigorous application of a single principle." He expressed this principle positively as: "Follow your reason as far as it will take you," and negatively as: "Do not pretend that conclusions are certain which are not demonstrated or demonstrable." This principle runs through the Western tradition: from Socrates, via the Reformation and the Enlightenment, to the axioms of modern science. Huxley called it the "agnostic faith."

First and foremost the Buddha taught a method ("dharma *practice*") rather than another "-ism." The dharma is not something to believe in but something to do. The Buddha did not reveal an esoteric set of facts about reality, which we can

choose to believe in or not. He challenged people to understand the nature of anguish, let go of its origins, realize its
cessation, and bring into being a way of life. The Buddha
followed his reason as far as it would take him and did not
pretend that any conclusion was certain unless it was demonstrable. Dharma practice has become a creed ("Buddhism")
much in the same way scientific method has degraded into
the creed of "Scientism."

JUST AS CONTEMPORARY agnosticism has tended to lose
its confidence and lapse into scepticism, so Buddhism has
tended to lose its critical edge and lapse into religiosity. What
each has lost, however, the other may be able to help restore.
In encountering contemporary culture, the dharma may recover its agnostic imperative, while secular agnosticism may
recover its soul.

An agnostic Buddhist would not regard the dharma as a
source of "answers" to questions of where we came from,
where we are going, what happens after death. He would
seek such knowledge in the appropriate domains: astro-
physics, evolutionary biology, neuroscience, etc. An agnostic
Buddhist is not a "believer" with claims to revealed information about supernatural or paranormal phenomena, and in
this sense is not "religious."

An agnostic Buddhist looks to the dharma for metaphors
of existential *confrontation* rather than metaphors of existential *consolation*. The dharma is not a belief by which you will
be miraculously saved. It is a method to be investigated and
tried out. It starts by facing up to the primacy of anguish,
then proceeds to apply a set of practices to understand the
human dilemma and work toward a resolution. The extent
to which dharma practice has been institutionalized as a
religion can be gauged by the number of consolatory ele-

ments that have crept in: for example, assurances of a better afterlife if you perform virtuous deeds or recite mantras or chant the name of a Buddha.

An agnostic Buddhist eschews atheism as much as theism, and is as reluctant to regard the universe as devoid of meaning as endowed with meaning. For to deny either God or meaning is simply the antithesis of affirming them. Yet such an agnostic stance is not based on disinterest. It is founded on a passionate recognition that *I do not know*. It confronts the enormity of having been born instead of reaching for the consolation of a belief. It strips away, layer by layer, the views that conceal the mystery of being here—either by affirming it as something or denying it as nothing.

Such deep agnosticism is an attitude toward life refined through ongoing mindful awareness. It may lead to the realization that ultimately there is neither something nor nothing at the core of ourselves that we can put a finger on. Or it may be focused in an intense perplexity that vibrates through the body and leaves the mind that seeks certainty nowhere to rest.

IN A FAMOUS parable the Buddha imagines a group of blind men who are invited to identify an elephant. One takes the tail and says it's a rope; another clasps a leg and says it's a pillar; another feels the side and says it's a wall; another holds the trunk and says it's a tube. Depending on which part of Buddhism you grasp, you might identify it as a system of ethics, a philosophy, a contemplative psychotherapy, a religion. While containing all of these, it can no more be reduced to any one of them than an elephant can be reduced to its tail.

That which contains the range of elements that constitute Buddhism is called a "culture." The term was first explicitly defined in 1871 by the anthropologist Sir Edward Burnett

Tylor as "that complex whole which includes knowledge, belief, art, morals, law, custom, and any other capabilities and habits acquired by man as a member of society." Since this particular culture originates in the awakening of Siddhartha Gautama and aims to cultivate a way of life conducive to such awakening, Buddhism could be described as "the culture of awakening."

While Buddhism has tended to become reductively identified with its religious forms, today it is in further danger of being reductively identified with its forms of meditation. If these trends continue, it is liable to become increasingly marginalized and lose its potential to be realized as a culture: an internally consistent set of values and practices that creatively animates all aspects of human life. The challenge now is to imagine and create a culture of awakening that both supports individual dharma practice and addresses the dilemmas of an agnostic and pluralist world.

# ANGUISH

*No conditions are permanent;*
*No conditions are reliable;*
*Nothing is self.*

—The Buddha

I T I S S A I D that until Siddhartha Gautama was in his late twenties, his father, King Suddhodana, kept him immured within palaces. Suddhodana did not wish his son to be distracted from his duty by the disquiet that reigned beyond the palace walls. The young man became restless in his incarceration and longed to go out. Suddhodana arranged tours of the town and countryside, making sure everything was perfectly arranged and nothing distressing passed before the boy's eyes. Despite these precautions, Siddhartha chanced upon a person disfigured by disease, another crippled by age, a corpse, and a wandering monk. He became uneasy upon returning to the comforts of home. One night he stole away. For six years he drifted around the land, studying, meditating, subjecting himself to punishing ascetic rigors. The conventional options exhausted, he sat down at the foot of a tree. Seven days later he had an awakening in which he understood the nature of anguish, let go of its origins, realized its cessation, and brought into being a way of life.

PRINCE SIDDHARTHA'S DILEMMA still faces us today. We too immure ourselves in the "palaces" of what is familiar and secure. We too sense that there is more to life than indulging desires and warding off fears. We too feel anguish most acutely when we break out of our habitual routines and witness ourselves hovering between birth and death—our birth and death. We discover that we have been thrown, apparently without choice, into a world not of our making. However painful the exit from the mother's uterus, it is mercifully forgotten. But in achieving consciousness, we realize that the only certainty in life is that it will end. We don't like the idea; we try to forget that too.

Everyone collaborates in everyone else's forgetting. Parents seek to prepare their offspring for life. Social and political institutions are there to benefit the living, not the dead. Religions largely offer consolation: perhaps there is a chance that we won't *really* die after all.

In one way or another, we manage to avoid the questions that existence raises, treating birth and death as physical events in time and space: the gasping of the first breath, the expelling of the last. They become isolated facts, problematic but manageable, kept at a distance from the here and now, where we are safe in the business of getting through the day.

Life becomes an exercise in the management of specifics.

We seek to arrange the details of our world in such a way that we feel secure: surrounded by what we like, protected against what we dislike. Once our material existence is more or less in order, we may turn our attention to the psychomanagement of our neuroses. Failing which, the worst anxieties can be kept at bay by a judicious use of drugs.

This approach works well enough until the unmanageable erupts again as sickness, aging, sorrow, pain, grief, despair. No matter how expertly we manage our lives, how convincing an image of well-being we project, we still find ourselves involved with what we hate and torn apart from what we love. We still don't get what we want and still get what we don't want. True, we experience joy, success, love, bliss. But in the end we find ourselves once more prone to anguish.

We may know this, but do we understand it? We see it, are even awed by it, but habit impels us to forget it. To cover it over and flee again to the lure of the tantalizing world. For were we to understand it, even in a glimpse, it might change everything.

Try this exercise. Find a quiet, comfortable place. This may be just the corner of a bedroom or study. Then settle into a chair or, if you prefer, sit cross-legged on a cushion on the floor. Make sure your back is unsupported and upright but not tense. Incline your head downward, so your gaze naturally falls about three feet in front of you.

Shut your eyes. Rest your hands in your lap or on your knees. Check to see if there are any points of tension in the body: the shoulders, the neck, around the eyes. Relax them. Become aware of your bodily contact with the ground. Make sure that you are steady and balanced. Notice the subtle polyphony of sounds around you, take note of any sensations in the body, be conscious of your mood of the moment. Don't judge these things or seek to change them: accept them for what they are.

Take three long, slow, deep breaths. Don't imagine the breath as some invisible stuff entering and leaving your nostrils; notice the bodily sensations (even the trivial ones like the shifting contact of your skin with your undershirt) that make up the act of breathing. Then let the breathing resume its own rhythm, without interfering with or controlling it. Just stay with it, letting the mind settle into the swell of the breath, like a small boat at anchor, gently rising and falling with the sea. Do this for ten minutes.

THIS EXERCISE MAY not be as straightforward as it seems. No matter how strong your resolve to be present and concentrated, it is difficult to keep the mind from wandering off into memories, plans, or fantasies. Several minutes may pass before you even *notice* that you have become distracted.

Normally we are unaware of the extent to which we are distracted, for the simple reason that distraction is a state of unawareness. This kind of exercise can force us to recognize that for much of the time we fail to register what is happening here and now. We are reliving an edited version of the past, planning an uncertain future, or indulging in being elsewhere. Or running on automatic pilot, without being conscious at all.

And instead of a coherent personality that stretches back in an unbroken line to a first memory and looks forward to an indefinite future, we discover a self ridden with gaps and ambiguities. Who "I am" appears coherent only because of the monologue we keep repeating, editing, censoring, and embellishing in our heads.

The present moment hovers between past and future just as life hovers between birth and death. We respond to both in similar ways. Just as we flee from the awesome encounter with birth and death to the safety of a manageable world, so we flee from the pulse of the present to a fantasy world. Flight is a reluctance to face change and the anguish it implies. Something in us insists on a static self, a fixed image, impervious to anguish, that will either survive death intact or be painlessly annihilated.

Evasion of the unadorned immediacy of life is as deep-seated as it is relentless. Even with the ardent desire to be aware and alert in the present moment, the mind flings us into tawdry and tiresome elaborations of past and future. This craving to be otherwise, to be elsewhere, permeates the body, feelings, perceptions, will—consciousness itself. It is like the background radiation from the big bang of birth, the aftershock of having erupted into existence.

SHOULD YOU PERSIST in watching the breath, you may find that after a while your mind begins to settle. You experience longer spells of concentration before a distracting thought whisks you away. You become more adept at remembering to come back to the present. You relax and discover a poignant tranquility. This is a centered stillness from which you can engage attentively, caringly, with the world.

All of life is in ceaseless mutation: emerging, modifying, disappearing. The relative constancy of still, centered attention is simply a steady adjustment to the flux of what is observed. Nothing can be relied upon for security. As soon as you grasp something, it's gone. Anguish emerges from craving for life to be other than it is. It is *the* symptom of flight from birth and death, from the pulse of the present. It is the gnawing mood of unease that haunts the clinging to "me" and "mine."

It would perhaps be better if life did not bring change—if

it could be relied upon to provide lasting happiness. But since this is not true, a calm and clear understanding of what is true—that no conditions are permanent or reliable—would weaken the grip in which craving holds us. Craving can vanish in awakening to the absurdity of the assumptions that underlie it. Without stamping it out or denying it, craving may be renounced the way a child renounces sandcastles: not by repressing the desire to make them but by turning aside from an endeavor that no longer holds any interest.

WHEN THE RESTLESS mind is stilled, we begin to encounter what is unfolding before us. This is both familiar and mysterious at the same time.

In one sense, we already know this world: in rare moments with nature, a lover, a work of art. Yet it also comes without warning: when strolling down a busy street, staring at a sheet of paper on a desk, forming a pot on a wheel. This sense of the world vanishes as suddenly as it appears. It is something we can neither manage nor control.

When we stop fleeing birth and death, the grip of anguish is loosened and existence reveals itself as a question. When Siddhartha encountered a person disfigured by disease, one crippled by age, a corpse, and a wandering monk, he was not only struck by the tragedy of anguish but thrown into questioning. Yet the questions he asked were not the sort he could stand back from, reflect on, and arrive at a rational answer to. He realized that he himself was subject to disease, aging, and death. The questioner was nothing other than the question itself. The pivotal moment of human consciousness: it becomes a question for itself.

Such a question is a mystery, not a problem. It cannot be "solved" by meditation techniques, through the authority of a text, upon submission to the will of a guru. Such strategies merely replace the question with beliefs in an answer.

As this kind of question becomes clearer it becomes more puzzling too. The understanding it generates does not provide consoling facts about the nature of life. This questioning probes ever deeper into what is still unknown.

# DEATH

*Like a dream,*
*Whatever I enjoy*
*Will become a memory;*
*The past is not revisited.*

—Shantideva

AGAIN FIND A comfortable place to sit, so that your back is upright, your body steady and balanced; then close your eyes and watch your breath. Feel the air enter your nostrils, expand your lungs and diaphragm. Pause, exhale, contracting diaphragm and lungs, then feel warmer air leave the nostrils. Sustain this attention for ten minutes, following each breath from beginning to end.

Reflect on your resolve: What has led me to this point? Why am I sitting here? Try not to get caught up in trains of associative thought that lead off into distraction. When the mind is calm and focused, consider this question:

*Since death alone is certain and the time of death uncertain, what should I do?*

Run this over in your mind, letting its import and challenge sink in. See if the question resonates in the body, triggers a nonverbal mood, a gut feeling. Give more attention to the bodily tone it evokes than to the thoughts and ideas it generates. If you feel such a tone, silently rest in it until it fades.

While you find the question intellectually stimulating, it might otherwise leave you cold. Or it may provoke only a pale hint of its implications. The aim of this meditation is to awaken a felt-sense of what it means to live a life that will stop. To deepen the question, the following reflections may help.

*Since death alone is certain . . .*

THINK OF THE beginnings of life on this earth: single-celled organisms dividing and evolving; the gradual emergence of fish, amphibians, and mammals, until the first human beings appeared around five million years ago; then the billions of men and women who preceded my own birth a mere handful of years ago. Each of them was born; each of them died. They died because they were born. What distinguishes me from any one of them? Did not they feel about the uniqueness of their lives just as I feel about the uniqueness of mine? Yet birth entails death as surely as meeting entails parting.

This miraculous organism, formed of an inconceivable number of interdependent parts, from the tiniest cell to the hemispheres of the brain, has evolved to a degree of complexity capable of the consciousness needed to make sense of these words. Life depends on sustaining this delicate balance, on the functioning of vital organs. Yet I feel it changing with each pulse of blood, slipping away with each breath. I witness my aging: the loss of hair, pain in the joints, wrinkling of skin. Life ebbs from moment to moment.

It is as though I am in a boat that floats steadily downstream. I gaze over the stern, admiring the landscape that spreads out behind the vessel. So absorbed am I in what I behold that I forget that I am drifting inexorably toward a waterfall that drops for hundreds of feet.

*... and the time of death uncertain ...*

WHEN I TRY to turn my head around to find how close the waterfall is, I cannot. I can see only what is unfolding before my eyes. I can see the death of others but not my own. The time will come for me too, but I don't know when.

Consider that while statistics assure us that we have a good chance to live to an "average" age, probability is not certainty. There can be no guarantee that I will live until next week, let alone for many years. Who do I know of my own age who has died? Was there anything about that person that made him a suitable candidate for a sudden or early death? How does he differ from me? I imagine myself in his shoes. Death does not happen only to others. Nor when I want it to.

This body is fragile. It is just flesh. Listen to the heartbeat. Life depends on the pumping of a muscle.

Anything can happen. Each time I cross a road, set out on a journey, descend a flight of stairs, my life is at risk. No matter how cautious I am, I cannot foresee the absentmindedness of the man in an approaching car, the collapse of a bridge, the shift of a fault line, the course of a stray bullet, the destination of a virus. Life is accident prone.

*. . . what should I do?*

WHAT AM I here for? Am I living in such a way that I can die without regrets? How much of what I do is compromise? Do I keep postponing what I "really" want to do until conditions are more favorable?

Asking such questions interrupts indulgence in the comforts of routine and shatters illusions about a cherished sense of self-importance. It forces me to seek again the impulse that moves me from the depths, and to turn aside from the shallows of habitual patterns. It requires that I examine my attachments to physical health, financial independence, loving friends. For they are easily lost; I cannot ultimately rely on them. Is there anything I can depend upon?

It might be that all I can trust in the end is my integrity to keep asking such questions as: *Since death alone is certain and the time of death uncertain, what should I do?* And then to act on them.

A REFLECTION LIKE this does not tell you anything you do not already know: that death is certain and its time uncertain. The point is to consider these facts regularly and slowly, allowing them to percolate through you, until a felt-sense of their meaning and implication is awakened. Even when you do this reflection daily, sometimes you may feel nothing at all; the thoughts may strike you as repetitive, shallow, and pointless. But at other times you may feel gripped by an urgent bodily awareness of imminent mortality. At such moments try to let the thoughts fade, and focus the entirety of your attention in this feeling.

This meditation counters the deep psychosomatic feeling

that there is something permanent at the core of ourself that is going to be around for a while yet. Intellectually, we may suspect such intuitions, but that is not how we feel most of the time. This feeling is not something that additional information or philosophy alone can affect. It needs to be challenged in its own terms.

Reflective meditation is a way of translating thoughts into the language of feeling. It explores the relation between the way we think about and perceive things and the way we feel about them. We find that even the strongest, seemingly self-evident intuitions about ourselves are based on equally deep-seated assumptions. Gradually learning to see our life in another way through reflective meditation leads to feeling different about it as well.

Ironically, we may discover that death meditation is not a morbid exercise at all. Only when we lose the use of something taken for granted (whether the telephone or an eye) are we jolted into a recognition of its value. When the phone is fixed, the bandage removed from the eye, we briefly rejoice in their restoration but swiftly forget them again. In taking them for granted, we cease to be conscious of them. In taking life for granted, we likewise fail to notice it. (To the extent that we get bored and long for something exciting to happen.) By meditating on death, we paradoxically become conscious of life.

How extraordinary it is to be here at all. Awareness of death can jolt us awake to the sensuality of existence. Breath is no longer a routine inhalation of air but a quivering intake of life. The eye is quickened to the play of light and shade and color, the ear to the intricate medley of sound. This is where the meditation leads. Stay with it; rest in it. Notice how distraction is a flight from this, an escape from awe to worry and plans.

AS THE MEDITATION draws to a close, return to your breath and posture. Open your eyes and slowly take in what you see in front of you. Before standing up and returning to other activities, reflect for a few moments on what you have noticed or learned.

These reflections may prepare us to encounter the actual death of others. The death of someone upsets the illusion of permanence we tacitly seek to sustain. Yet we are skilled in disguising such reactions with expressions and conventions that contain death within a manageable social frame. To meditate on the certainty of death and the uncertainty of its time helps transform the experience of another's death from an awkward discomfiture into an awesome and tragic con-clusion to the transience that lies at the heart of all life.

Over time such meditation penetrates our primary sense of being in the world at all. It helps us value more deeply our relationships with others, whom we come to regard as tran-sient as ourselves. It evokes the poignancy implicit in the transitoriness of all things.

# REBIRTH

*"But if there is no other world and there is no fruit and ripening of actions well done or ill done, then here and now in this life I shall be free from hostility, affliction, and anxiety, and I shall live happily." This is the second comfort acquired....*

—The Buddha

ELIGIONS ARE UNITED not by belief in God but by belief in life after death. According to religious Buddhism we will be reborn in a form of life that accords with the ethical quality of actions committed in this or a previous life. A similar principle is followed in the monotheistic religions, although the postmortem options tend to be limited to heaven or hell. Throughout history, religions have explained that death is not the end of life but that some part of us—perhaps all of us—carries on.

The Buddha accepted the idea of rebirth. It is said that as

34

part of his awakening he recalled the entire chain of births that preceded the present one. Later he described, sometimes in detail, how actions committed in the past determine experiences in this life and how actions committed now will determine the quality of one's afterlife. He spoke of the process of awakening in terms of how many rebirths remain until a person is freed from the cycle of compulsive birth and death. Although he taught dharma practice to be meaningful whether or not we believe in rebirth, and speculation about future and past lives to be just another distraction, the evidence does not suggest that he held an agnostic view on the matter.

Yet while religions may agree that life continues in some form after death, this does not indicate the claim to be true. Until quite recently religions maintained that the earth was flat, but such widespread belief did not affect the shape of the planet. In accepting the idea of rebirth, the Buddha reflected the worldview of his time. In common with Indian tradition, he maintained that the aim of life is to attain freedom from the anguished cycle of compulsive rebirth. (It's a curious twist that Westerners find the idea of rebirth consoling.) This view was endorsed by subsequent generations of Buddhists in much the same way as we would now endorse many scientific views, which, if pressed, we would find hard to demonstrate.

The Buddha found the prevailing Indian view of rebirth sufficient as a basis for his ethical and liberating teaching. Subsequently, religious Buddhism emphasized that denial of rebirth would undermine the basis of ethical responsibility and the need for morality in society. Similar fears were expressed at the time of the Enlightenment by the Christian churches, who feared that loss of faith in heaven and hell would lead to rampant immorality. One of the great realizations of the Enlightenment was that an atheistic materialist could be just as moral a person as a believer—even more so. This insight led to liberation from the constraints of ecclesiastical dogma, which was crucial in forming the sense of intellectual and political freedom we enjoy today.

❧

IT IS OFTEN claimed that you cannot be a Buddhist if you do not accept the doctrine of rebirth. From a traditional point of view, it is indeed problematic to suspend belief in the idea of rebirth, since many basic notions then have to be re-thought. But if we follow the Buddha's injunction not to accept things blindly, then orthodoxy should not stand in the way of forming our own understanding.

A difficulty that has beset Buddhism from the beginning is the question of what it is to be reborn. Religions that posit an eternal self distinct from the body-mind complex escape this dilemma—the body and mind may die but the self continues. A central Buddhist idea, however, is that no such intrinsic self can be found through analysis or realized in meditation. Such a deep-seated sense of personal identity is a fiction, a tragic habit that lies at the root of craving and anguish. How do we square this with rebirth, which necessarily entails the existence of something that not only survives the death of the body and brain but somehow traverses the space between a corpse and a fertilized ovum?

Different Buddhist schools have come up with different answers to this question, which in itself suggests their views are based on speculation. Some claim that the force of habit-driven craving immediately reappears in another form of life; others posit various kinds of nonphysically based mental consciousness that may spend several weeks before locating a suitable womb.

These kinds of speculations lead us far from the Buddha's agnostic and pragmatic perspective and into a consideration of metaphysical views that cannot be demonstrated or re-futed, proven or disproven. Even if irrefutable evidence for rebirth were to appear one day, it would only raise other, more difficult questions. The mere fact of rebirth would not entail any ethical linkage between one existence and the next. Demonstrating that death will be followed by another life is not the same as demonstrating that a murderer will be reborn in hell and a saint in heaven.

The idea of rebirth is meaningful in religious Buddhism only insofar as it provides a vehicle for the key Indian metaphysical doctrine of actions and their results known as "karma." While the Buddha accepted the idea of karma as he accepted that of rebirth, when questioned on the issue he tended to emphasize its psychological rather than its cosmological implications. "Karma," he often said, "is intention": i.e., a movement of the mind that occurs each time we think, speak, or act. By being mindful of this process, we come to understand how intentions lead to habitual patterns of behavior, which in turn affect the quality of our experience. In contrast to the view often taught by religious Buddhists, he denied that karma alone was sufficient to explain the origin of individual experience.

All this has nothing to do, however, with the compatibility (or otherwise) of Buddhism and modern science. It is odd that a practice concerned with anguish and the ending of anguish should be obliged to adopt ancient Indian metaphysical theories and thus accept as an article of faith that consciousness cannot be explained in terms of brain function. Dharma practice can never be in contradiction with science: not because it provides some mystical validation of scientific findings but because it simply is not concerned with either validating or invalidating them. Its concern lies entirely with the nature of existential experience.

❧

WHERE DOES THIS leave us? It may seem that there are two options: either to believe in rebirth or not. But there is a third alternative: to acknowledge, in all honesty, *I do not know*. We neither have to adopt the literal versions of rebirth presented by religious tradition nor fall into the extreme of regarding death as annihilation. Regardless of what we believe, our actions will reverberate beyond our deaths. Irrespective of our personal survival, the legacy of our thoughts, words, and deeds will continue through the impressions we leave behind in the lives of those we have influenced or touched in any way.

Dharma practice requires the courage to confront what it means to be human. All the pictures we entertain of heaven and hell or cycles of rebirth serve to replace the unknown with an image of what is already known. To cling to the idea of rebirth can deaden questioning.

Failure to summon forth the courage to risk a nondogmatic and nonevasive stance on such crucial existential matters can also blur our ethical vision. If our actions in the world are to stem from an encounter with what is central in life, they must be unclouded by either dogma or prevarication. Agnosticism is no excuse for indecision. If anything, it is a catalyst for action; for in shifting concern away from a future life and back to the present, it demands an ethics of empathy rather than a metaphysics of fear and hope.

# RESOLVE

*When crows find a dying snake,*
*They behave as if they were eagles.*
*When I see myself as a victim,*
*I am hurt by trifling failures.*

—Shantideva

LIFE IS NEITHER meaningful nor meaningless. Meaning and its absence are given to life by language and imagination. We are linguistic beings who inhabit a reality in which it makes sense to make sense.

For life to make sense it needs purpose. Even if our aim in life is to be totally in the here and now, free from past conditioning and any idea of a goal to be reached, we still have a clear purpose—without which life would be meaningless. A purpose is formed of words and images. And we can no more step out of language and imagination than we can step out of our bodies.

THE PROBLEM IS not that we lack resolve, but that it so often turns out to be misplaced. The meaning-laden feelings do not last. We resolve to become wealthy and famous, only to discover in the end that such things are incapable of providing that permanent well-being we initially projected onto them. Wealth and success are all very well; but once we have them their allure fades. It is like climbing a mountain. We expend great energy and hope on reaching the top, only to find when we get there that it is dwarfed by another even higher ridge.

In a changing, ambiguous world is anything worthy of total commitment? It is tempting to appeal to a purpose-giving God outside of time and space, a transcendent Absolute in which ultimate meaning is secured. But is this appeal not an urge for the consolation of religion? Is it not falling prey to the bewitchment of language? Dharma practice starts not with belief in a transcendent reality but through embracing the anguish experienced in an uncertain world.

A purpose may be no more than a set of images and words, but we can still be totally committed to it. Such resolve entails aspiration, appreciation, and conviction: I aspire to awaken, I appreciate its value, and I am convinced it is possible. This is a focused act that encompasses the whole person. Aspiration is as much a bodily longing as an intellectual desire; appreciation as much a passion as a preference; conviction as much an intuition as a rational conclusion. Irrespective of the purpose to which we are committed, when such feelings are aroused, life is infused with meaning.

ANGUISH EMERGES FROM craving for life to be other than it is. In the face of a changing world, such craving seeks consolation in something permanent and reliable, in a self that is in control of things, in a God who is in charge of destiny. The irony of this strategy is that it turns out to be the cause of what it seeks to dispel. In yearning for anguish to be assuaged in such ways, we reinforce what creates anguish in the first place: the craving for life to be other than it is. We find ourselves spinning in a vicious circle. The more acute the anguish, the more we want to be rid of it, but the more we want to be rid of it, the more acute it gets.

Such behavior is not just a silly mistake we can shrug off. It is an ingrained habit, an addiction. It persists even when we are aware of its self-destructive nature. To counter it requires resolve of equivalent force to live in another way. This is unlikely, though, to lead to an immediate change in the way we feel. A smoker may fervently resolve to give up cigarettes, but that does not prevent the tug of longing each time he enters a smoke-filled room. What changes is his resolve.

Dharma practice is founded on resolve. This is not an emotional conversion, a devastating realization of the error of our ways, a desperate urge to be good, but an ongoing, heartfelt reflection on priorities, values, and purpose. We need to keep taking stock of our life in an unsentimental, uncompromising way.

SOMEONE MIGHT SAY: "I resolve to awaken, to practice a way of life conducive to that end, and to cultivate friendships that nurture it," but he may feel exactly the opposite much of the time. We are often content to drift from day to day, follow routines, indulge habits, and hang out, dimly aware of the background echo of our deeper resolve. We know this is insincere, unsatisfying—yet still do it. Even in meditation we may go through the mechanics of practice, lapse into fantasies, get bored. Or become self-righteous and pious.

Awakening is the purpose that enfolds all purposes. Whatever we do is meaningful to the extent that it leads to awakening, meaningless to the extent that it leads away from it. Dharma practice is the process of awakening itself: the thoughts, words, and deeds that weave the unfolding fabric of experience into a coherent whole. And this process is participatory: sustained and matured by communities of friendships.

The process of awakening is like walking on a footpath. When we find such a path after hours of struggling through undergrowth, we know at last that we are heading somewhere. Moreover, we suddenly find that we can move freely without obstruction. We settle into a rhythmic and easy pace. At the same time we are reconnected to others: men, women, and animals who have walked here before us. The path is maintained as a path only because of the tread of feet. Just as others have created this path for us, so by walking on it we maintain it for those who will come after us. What counts is not so much the destination but the resolve to take the next step.

Treading the path of awakening can embrace a range of purposes. At times we may concentrate on the specifics of material existence: creating a livelihood that is in accord with our deepest values and aspirations. At times we may retreat: disentangling ourselves from social and psychological pressures in order to reconsider our life in a quiet and supportive setting. At times we may engage with the world: responding empathetically and creatively to the anguish of others.

There is no hierarchy among these purposes; one is not "better" than the other; we do not "progress" from one to the next. They each have their time and place. If we seek inner detachment and clarity while our outer life is a mess, we may enjoy periodic escapes from turmoil but find no lasting equanimity. If we devote ourselves to the welfare of the world

while our inner life is riven by irrational ideals and unre-
solved compulsions, we can easily undermine our own resolve.

COMMITMENT TO THE most worthy purpose is of little
value if we lack confidence in our ability to realize it. We may
console ourselves with the idea that at some future time
awakening will dawn as a reward for having believed in it
long enough. This is to literalize purpose: to confuse a valu-
able aim with an entity endowed with a shadowy, metaphysical existence. The longing for consolation might run deeper
than we like to admit. It enables us to feel good about
ourselves without having to do a great deal. But can we
afford the luxury of consolation in a world where death is the
only certainty, its time utterly uncertain, and the hereafter a
hypothesis?

A commitment to dharma practice keeps us on our toes.
We can notice when our resolve eases into a complacent
routine, and observe how we seek to justify ourselves by
seeking approval from others. We can be conscious of how
we tend to ignore or escape anguish rather than understand
and accept it. We can be aware that even when we gain
insight into these things, we rarely behave differently in the
future. Despite our overt resolve, we are still creatures of
habit.

Resolve is activated by self-confidence, which in turn depends on the kind of self-image we have. If we see ourselves
as insignificant, always in the shadow of others, then the
slightest hardship will seem daunting. We will be drawn to
those who insist that awakening is a distant goal, accessible
only to a privileged few. Conversely, if we see ourselves as
superior to others, then while outwardly disdainful of hardship, we are tormented by humiliation when it defeats us. We

shun the friendship of those who might help dispel the conceit that traps us in yet another cycle of anguish.

Self-confidence is not a form of arrogance. It is trust in our capacity to awaken. It is both the courage to face whatever life throws at us without losing equanimity, and the humility to treat every situation we encounter as one from which we can learn.

# INTEGRITY

*A monk asked Yun Men, "What are the teachings of a whole
lifetime?" Yun Men said, "An appropriate statement."*

—*The Blue Cliff Record*

T HE RESOLVE TO awaken requires the integrity not to
hurt anyone in the process. Dharma practice cannot be
abstracted from the way we interact with the world. Our
deeds, words, and intentions create an ethical ambience that
either supports or weakens resolve. If we behave in a way
that harms either others or ourselves, the capacity to focus on
the task will be weakened. We'll feel disturbed, distracted,
uneasy. The practice will have less effect, as though the
vitality of resolve is being drained.

Ethical integrity is rooted in the sense of who we are and

what kind of reality we inhabit. That we are isolated, anxious creatures in a hostile world may not be a conscious philosophical view but a gut feeling buried beneath the image of the compassionate and responsible person projected to the world. Only when one is frightened or overwhelmed by greed or hate is this underlying attitude revealed. Then each one experiences himself pitted against the rest of the world: one desperate soul struggling to survive among others.

There are many ways to hurt others when we feel like this: from killing or injuring them physically, or depriving them of what is rightfully theirs to abusing or taking advantage of them sexually; from lying to them, speaking unkindly about them behind their backs, or uttering cruel and barbed remarks to wasting their time with senseless chatter. Integrity entails not merely refraining from overt acts of this kind, but also recognizing how we contemplate such behavior in our thoughts, repeat it through fantasy, or prepare for it even though we lose our nerve before carrying it out.

THERE ARE ALSO moments when we experience ourselves not at odds with others but as participants in a shared reality. As empathetic beings in a participatory reality we cannot, without losing our integrity, hurt, abuse, rob, or lie to others.

Ethical integrity originates in empathy, for then we take the well-being of others to heart and are moved to be generous and caring. Our thoughts, words, and deeds are based on a sense of what we have in common rather than what divides us. But just because we feel deeply for someone's plight and are motivated by the noblest intentions, this does not ensure that what we do will be for the best. Empathy alone will not prevent us from making mistakes.

While rooted in empathy, integrity requires courage and intelligence as well, because every significant ethical choice entails risk. And while we cannot know in advance the consequences of the choices we make, we can learn to become more ethically intelligent.

Ethical intelligence is cultivated by learning from concrete mistakes. We can discern when a reactive habit kicks in and prompts us to adopt the familiar path of least resistance. We can notice when empathy capitulates to fear or self-interest. We can be alert for face-saving words and gestures that give an impression of empathy while letting us off the hook. And we can recognize when we are evading the crises of risk.

How often do we refrain from acting, out of fear of how our actions might be received? To let such a moment slip away can be agonizing. To combat such fear requires the courage to live in a less self-centered and more compassionate way. However daunting a situation may seem, as soon as we say or do something, it is suddenly transformed. When the door of hesitation is unlocked, we enter a dynamic, fluid world, which challenges us to act and act again.

The most soul-searching meditation on ethics leaves the world intact; a single word or deed can transform it forever.

ETHICAL INTEGRITY REQUIRES both the intelligence to understand the present situation as the fruition of former choices, and the courage to engage with it as the arena for the creation of what is to come. It empowers us to embrace the ambiguity of a present that is simultaneously tied to an irrevocable past and free for an undetermined future.

Ethical integrity is not moral certainty. A priori certainty about right and wrong is at odds with a changing and unreliable world, where the future lies open, waiting to be born from choices and acts. Such certainty may be consoling and strengthening, but it can blunt awareness of the uniqueness of each ethical moment. When we are faced with the unprecedented and unrepeatable complexities of this moment, the question is not "What is the right thing to do?" but "What is the compassionate thing to do?" This question can be approached with integrity but not with certainty. In accepting that every action is a risk, integrity embraces the fallibility that certainty disdainfully eschews.

Ethical integrity is threatened as much by attachment to the security of what is known as by fear of the insecurity of what is unknown. It is liable to be remorselessly buffetted by the winds of desire and fear, doubt and worry, fantasy and egoism. The more we give in to these things, the more our integrity is eroded and we find ourselves carried along on a wave of psychological and social habit. When responding to a moral dilemma, we just repeat the gestures and words of a parent, an authority figure, a religious text. While moral conditioning may be necessary for social stability, it is inadequate as a paradigm of integrity.

Occasionally, though, we act in a way that startles us. A friend asks our advice about a tricky moral choice. Yet instead of offering him consoling platitudes or the wisdom of someone else, we say something that we did not know we knew. Such gestures and words spring from body and tongue with shocking spontaneity. We cannot call them "mine" but neither have we copied them from others. Compassion has dissolved the stranglehold of self. And we taste, for a few exhilarating seconds, the creative freedom of awakening.

# FRIENDSHIP

*Just as the dawn is the forerunner of the arising of the sun, so true friendship is the forerunner of the arising of the noble eightfold path.*

—The Buddha

DHARMA PRACTICE IS not just a question of cultivating resolve and integrity in the privacy of our
hearts. It is embodied in friendships. Our practice is nour-
ished, sustained, and challenged through ongoing contact
with friends and mentors who seek to realize the dharma in
their own lives.

We were born alone and will die alone. Much of our time
is spent absorbed in feelings and thoughts we can never fully
share. Yet our lives are nonetheless defined through relationships with others. The body is witness to parents and endless

generations of forebears, language witness to fellow speakers, the most private thoughts witness to those we love and fear. Simultaneously and always, we find ourselves alone with others.

We are participatory beings who inhabit a participatory reality, seeking relationships that enhance our sense of what it means to be alive. In terms of dharma practice, a true friend is more than just someone with whom we share common values and who accepts us for what we are. Such a friend is someone whom we can trust to refine our understanding of what it means to live, who can guide us when we're lost and help us find the way along a path, who can assuage our anguish through the reassurance of his or her presence.

WHILE SUCH FRIENDSHIPS occur naturally between peers with similar aspirations and interests, certain crucial friendships are also formed with those we respect for having achieved a maturity and understanding greater than our own. Such people offer guidance and reassurance through each aspect of their being. The way they move their body and hold our gaze with their eyes, the cadences of their speech, their response to sudden provocation, the way they rest at ease and attend to daily chores: all these things tell us as much as they tell us in words. And we too are called upon to respond in such ways. In this kind of relationship we are no mere recipients of knowledge. We are invited to interact, to challenge and be challenged.

These friends are teachers in the sense that they are skilled in the art of learning from every situation. We do not seek perfection in these friends but rather heartfelt acceptance of human imperfection. Nor omniscience but an ironic admission of ignorance. We should be wary of being seduced by charismatic purveyors of Enlightenment. For true friends seek not to coerce us, even gently and reasonably, into believing what we are unsure of. These friends are like midwives, who draw forth what is waiting to be born. Their task is not to make themselves indispensable but redundant.

These friends are our vital link to past and future. For they too were nurtured through friendships, in many cases with those who are dead. Dharma practice has survived through a series of friendships that stretches back through history— ultimately to Gautama himself. Through friendships we are entrusted with a delicate thread that joins past with future generations. These fragile, intimate moments are ones of indebtedness and responsibility. Dharma practice flourishes only when such friendships flourish. It has no other means of transmission.

And these friends are our vital links to a community that lives and struggles today. Through them we belong to a culture of awakening, a matrix of friendships, that expands in ever wider circles to embrace not only "Buddhists" but all who are actually or potentially committed to the values of dharma practice.

THE FORMS OF this friendship have changed over history. The dharma has passed through social and ethnic cultures with different ideals of what constitutes true friendship. Two primary forms have emerged: the fellowship model of early Buddhism and the guru-disciple model of later traditions. In both cases, friendship has become entangled with issues of religious authority.

Before the Buddha died he declared that the dharma would suffice as one's guide. In the early community, friendship was founded in common adherence to the rules of discipline the Buddha devised to support dharma practice. The community was a fellowship of brotherhood and sisterhood, under the formal guidance of a paternal or maternal preceptor. While the system reflected the hierarchy of an Indian extended family, in which everyone deferred to seniority, the final authority lay not in a person's position in the hierarchy but in the rules of discipline. True friendship was modeled on the relationships among siblings and between child and parent, with the difference that all were equal in the eyes of the dharma and subject to its law.

After about five hundred years, the Indian guru-disciple model was adopted by certain schools. Here the teacher became a heroic figure to whose will the student surrendered as a means of accelerating the process of awakening. This relationship reflected that between master and servant or feudal lord and subject. The different degree of power between guru and disciple was utilized as an agent of personal transformation. Elements of dominance and submission (and with them the concomitant danger of coercion) came to characterize the notion of true friendship. If, after close examination, you accepted someone as your teacher, then you were expected to revere and obey him. In varying degrees, the authority of the dharma was replaced by the authority of the guru, who came, in some traditions, to assume the role of the Buddha himself.

Despite the contrasting nature of these models, in practice they coexisted. As a follower of the Buddha's rules of discipline, a true friend was accountable to the community and the dharma, but as a guru was impervious to any critique formulated by the deluded mind. Most traditions of Buddhism today represent one of these ideals of friendship or a blend of the two.

IN CONTEMPORARY SECULAR, democratic societies, such traditional models of friendship are bound to be challenged.

For we may no longer feel at ease in friendships defined by the hierarchy of an extended family, the rule of law, or submission to the will of another. We may no longer feel the need to wear a uniform or in any way sacrifice our ordinariness. Exotic names, robes, insignia of office, titles—the trappings of religion—confuse as much as they help. They endorse the assumption of the existence of an elite whose explicit commitment grants them implicit extraordinariness.

It is not just different circumstances that raise questions about the nature of true friendship. Of greater significance is that we *notice* that circumstances are different. Historical consciousness itself makes the difference. It is no longer possible to maintain that dharma practice has remained unaltered since the time of the Buddha. It has evolved and continues to evolve distinctive forms peculiar to the conditions of the time. It has survived precisely because of its ability to respond creatively to change.

What features of contemporary life are most likely to affect the concept of true friendship? Mutual respect for the creative autonomy of individual experience would take precedence over submission to the dogmas of a school or the autocratic authority of a guru. The responsibility of a friend would be to encourage individuation, self-reliance, and imagination. Such friendship might be informed by notions such as Martin Buber's "I-Thou" relationship and the French Catholic philosopher Gabriel Marcel's ideal of "availability" for another. Its practice may draw on the experience of psychotherapy, in which a "free and protective space" allows an encounter that is simultaneously trusting, opening, and healing. For learning and training, it may take as its model the relationship of artist and apprentice, in which skills are developed so that creativity can be realized with technical competence and expertise.

Whenever Buddhism has become a religion, true friendship has tended to be compromised by issues of power. Both the fellowship and guru-disciple models have given rise to large, impersonal, hierarchic, and authoritarian bodies governed by professional elites. In many cases, these institutions have become established churches, sanctioned and supported by sovereign states. This has often led to rigid conservativism and intolerance of dissent.

This process is not inevitable. It is also possible to imagine a community of friendships in which diversity is celebrated rather than censured. In which smallness of scale is regarded as success rather than failure. In which power is shared by all rather than invested in a minority of experts. In which women and men are treated as genuine equals. In which questions are valued more than answers.

# PATH

*One day an old man was circumambulating Reting Monastery. Geshe Drom said to him: "Sir, I am happy to see you circumambulating, but wouldn't you prefer to be practicing the dharma?"*

*Thinking this over, the old man felt he'd better cover himself by reading some Buddhist scriptures. While he was reading in the temple courtyard, Geshe Drom said: "I am happy to see you reading the dharma, but wouldn't you prefer to be practicing it?"*

*At this, the old man thought that the best way to cover himself would be to meditate single pointedly. He put aside his reading and sat on a cushion, his eyes half-closed. Drom said: "Good to see you meditating, but wouldn't you rather be practicing the dharma?"*

*With nothing else left to do, the old man asked: "Geshe-la, please, how should I practice the dharma?"*

*"When you practice," Drom replied, "there is no distinction between the dharma and your own mind."*

—Tsun ba je gom

*Miscellaneous Advice of the Kadampa Masters*

# AWARENESS

*And further, a monk knows when he is going, "I am going."*
*He knows when he is standing, "I am standing." He knows*
*when he is sitting, "I am sitting." He knows when he is lying*
*down, "I am lying down."*

—The Buddha

I OPEN THE refrigerator to discover that I have no milk and so decide to go down to the store to get some. I shut the door behind me, turn left into the street, follow the sidewalk for two blocks, turn left and left again, enter the store, snatch a carton of milk from the shelf, pay for it at the checkout, leave the store, turn right and right again, go back along the sidewalk for two blocks, turn right, unlock the door, and go back into the kitchen.

The only evidence I have that any of this has happened is the cold carton of milk now clutched rather too firmly in my hand.

As I try to reconstruct those ten vanished minutes, I recall being engrossed in a memory of something S said to me yesterday that I have been shrugging off ever since. It irked me and has become lodged as a stab of disquiet somewhere in the upper part of my stomach. I can remember that as I walked along, I was absorbed in what I should have said when the remark was made and what I would say were it repeated. The exact words of my response escape me. But I recall feeling gratified by their sharp blend of insouciance and cruelty, confirmed, in my imagination, by the look of fear on S's face as he is pinned to a rough wooden floor.

As for the first chill hint of winter in the gust of wind that sent the last withered leaves scratching along the sidewalk before me as I pulled my warm collar tight against the skin of my neck, I have no recollection. And although I was staring intently in S's direction, I failed to notice the waving arm of my friend perched on his bicycle across the street, his call and whistle, his smile as he rode off when the light turned green.

MUCH OF OUR time is spent like this. As we become aware of it we begin to suspect that we are not entirely in control of our lives. Much of the time we are driven by a relentless and insistent surge of impulses. We notice this in quiet moments of reflection, but usually just get carried along on the crest of its wave. Until, that is, we crash once more onto the rocks of recriminatory self-consciousness, and from there into moods and depressions.

One of the most difficult things to remember is to remember to remember. Awareness begins with remembering what we tend to forget. Drifting through life on a cushioned surge of impulses is but one of many strategies of forgetting. Not only do we forget to remember, we forget that we live in a body with senses and feelings and thoughts and emotions and ideas. Worrying about what a friend said can preoccupy us so completely that it isolates us from the rest of our experience. The world of colors and shapes, sounds, smells, tastes, and sensations becomes dull and remote. Even the person who offers sympathy appears alien and out of reach. We feel cut off and adrift.

To stop and pay attention to what is happening in the moment is one way of snapping out of such fixations. It is also a reasonable definition of meditation.

WHILE MEDITATION MAY be cultivated as a formal practice once or twice a day for half an hour or so, the aim is to bring a fresh awareness into everything we do. Whether walking or standing still, sitting or lying down, alone or in company, resting or working, I try to maintain that same careful attention. So when I go to get milk, I will notice the scratching sound of the leaves on the sidewalk as well as my anger and hurt at what S said.

Awareness is a process of deepening self-acceptance. It is neither a cold, surgical examination of life nor a means of becoming perfect. Whatever it observes, it embraces. There is nothing unworthy of acceptance. The light of awareness will doubtless illuminate things we would prefer not to see. And this may entail a descent into what is forbidden, repressed, denied. We might uncover disquieting memories, irrational childhood terrors. We might have to accept not only a potential sage hidden within but also a potential murderer, rapist, or thief.

Despite the sense I might have of myself as a caring person, I observe that I want to punch S in the face. What usually happens to this hatred? I restrain myself from expressing it, not out of any great love for S but because of how it would affect other people's view of me. The attachment to self-image likewise inclines me to shy away from and forget this viciousness. In one way or another I deny it. I do not allow it into the field of awareness. I do not embrace it.

Or I may play it out as a fantasy, either in my imagination or on the analyst's couch. This may temporarily relieve the symptoms of rage and frustration, but will it make a difference when S presents me with his next barbed remark? Probably not. Such fantasies might even reinforce the kind of emotions they seek to assuage. As the hatred rears up again, something in me knows immediately how to relieve it. This becomes a habit that demands ever larger doses of anger to enjoy relief from. I could develop a subtle taste for violence. I might even end up by hitting S.

But to embrace hatred does not mean to indulge it. To embrace hatred is to accept it for what it is: a disruptive but transient state of mind. Awareness observes it jolt into being, coloring consciousness and gripping the body. The heart accelerates, the breath becomes shallow and jagged, and an almost physical urge to react dominates the mind. At the same time, this frenzy is set against a dark, quiet gulf of hurt, humiliation, and shame. Awareness notices all this without condoning or condemning, repressing or express-ing. It recognizes that just as hatred arises, so will it pass away.

By identifying with it ("I really am *pissed off!*"), we fuel it. Not that we consciously choose to do so. The impulsive surge has such an abrupt momentum that by the time we first notice the anger, identification has already occurred. Sud-denly we realize that we are perspiring, the heart is beating faster, hurtful words are choking in the throat, and our fists are clenched. By that time there is little we can do but watch the anger buffet and batter us. The task of awareness is to catch the impulse at its inception, to notice the very first hint of resentment coloring our feelings and perceptions. But such precision requires a focused mind.

FOCUSED AWARENESS IS both calm and clear. Just as calmness is prevented by restlessness and distraction, so clarity is undermined by boredom and lethargy. Drifting between these two poles, we spend much of our time either slightly hyper or slightly depressed.

Restlessness is like a monkey swinging from branches and crashing through foliage. When in its grip, we suffer a compelling urgency to be elsewhere: if I am in, I want to go out; if I am out, I want to come in. We feel imprisoned. Even if we manage to settle down physically, the mind runs amok. No sooner have we started meditating than we're off chasing chimeras. Instead of contemplating life and death, I struggle to remember the name of Led Zeppelin's drummer.

Distraction drugs us into forgetfulness. Even when we yearn to be focused on something meaningful, it erupts again. We cannot switch it off—and the more frustrated we get, the worse it becomes.

Instead of fighting it, embrace it. Accept that this is how things are right now: I am compulsively distracted. Acceptance might even lead to understanding what it is that we're running from. Instead of giving in to irritation, gently and patiently keep bringing the attention back. Then we may suddenly notice that the turmoil has stopped, as though a storm has passed. There might still be an occasional gust, but—for the time being, at least—it is calm.

Of course no sooner does calm establish itself than the doldrums are likely to set in. Distraction is replaced by boredom. Instead of an excess of energy, we feel drained. We want to collapse somewhere, lie down, doze, and sleep. Our thoughts are fuzzy, unwieldy, trapped in a mental fog. This might be just physical exhaustion, in which case a nap would do the trick. But if it doesn't, then this sleepiness might be the dark shadow of restlessness: another strategy of evasion. It's easy to tell: when the phone rings or lunch is announced, such tiredness suddenly vanishes.

No amount of meditative expertise from the mystical East will solve this problem, because such restlessness and lethargy are not mere mental or physical lapses but reflexes of an existential condition. Focused awareness is difficult not because we are inept at some spiritual technology but because it threatens our sense of who we are. The apparently unthreatening act of settling the mind on the breath and observing what is occurring in the body and mind exposes a contradiction between the sort of person we wish to be and the kind of person we are. Restlessness and lethargy are ways of evading the discomfort of this contradiction.

At such times, it may be futile to try to force the attention back to the object of meditation. Instead, we need to clarify the resolve that underpins dharma practice. We need to reflect on our motive, asking ourself: "Why I am doing this?" Or we may consider the certainty of death and the uncertainty of its time, concluding with the question: "What should I do?" Such reflections can help ground us in the very reality that restlessness and lethargy are so keen to avoid.

When centered in a clear and firm resolve, remembering to be aware can lead to a focused awareness that permeates every aspect of experience. What started as occasional moments of recollection develops into moment-to-moment mindfulness. This is not to say we never suffer from bouts of excitement or lethargy, but it is possible for consciousness to become increasingly wakeful.

FIND A QUIET, comfortable place. Sit still. Make sure the back is unsupported and upright, but not tense. Check to see if there are any points of tension in the body: the shoulders, the neck, around the eyes. Relax them. Take three long, slow, deep breaths. Then let the breathing resume its own rhythm, without interference or control.

The formal practice of mindfulness begins with a heightened awareness of the sensory array that is the body. Central to this is breathing. When meditating on the breath, let go of any picture you have of some invisible stuff being sucked in then pumped out of the lungs. Likewise, if you have an image of the meditating self peering down on the breath from above the head, let that go too. Experience the breath as the body experiences it: a rhythm of sensations that starts with the impact of cool indrawn air on the opening of the nostrils and ends with a warmer current leaving that same point moments later. Only when you start paying careful attention to the breath do you notice how complex and subtle are the range of sensations involved. As each inhalation and exhalation takes place, delve deeper into the multilayered intricacy of this vital act.

When you become calm, centered, and alert to the breath, slowly expand awareness to include whatever other bodily sensations are present. Focus your attention on the crown of the head, then calmly and patiently move over every detail of your scalp, face, and neck, through the torso and limbs, to the tips of your toes. Again: don't picture these things to yourself but experience them sensually as warmth or coolness, heaviness, tension, motion, tingling, itching. Notice any areas where sensation is absent and probe them too.

While our mental picture of the body may be idealized and fixed (a version of how we pose to ourselves in a mirror), the sensous experience of the body is one of complex, interconnected processes that never remain the same for a moment. Nor are these processes just physical. In concert they reflect our emotional state of the moment: content, sad, buoyant, depressed. Specific points in the body (gut, solar plexus, heart, throat) especially concentrate knots of emotion. Every mental state is also known through a corresponding physical sensation. It is as though this body is a tree alive with scurrying feelings, rustling ideas, chattering thoughts, chirping intuitions.

Then suddenly we are no longer in touch with these experiences. A memory, a fantasy, a fear has snatched us away into the dim, seductive twilight of unawareness. We mentally blink, and the fascinating array of sensations vanishes. A single moment of forgetfulness lets the surge of impulses rush in again and sweep us away. Minutes pass before we even notice that we are distracted. We come back with a shock: our thoughts are racing (although we may have already forgotten why), our heart pumping, our forehead sweating. We return shakily to the breath.

The practice of mindfulness entails patiently returning to the object of meditation again and again. Once the breath has settled, we can expand awareness once more to bodily sensations, feelings, emotions, thoughts, until the mind is calm and clear enough to detect the very first hint of a disturbing impulse. But it is not enough just to detect it. We need the resolve to resist savoring the memory or fantasy for just a few delectable moments before letting it go. For once it has you under its sway—even for a moment—it will whisk you off again.

Mindfulness is not only introspective. Once inner calm and clarity are present, expand your attention to the world around you: the medley of sounds that continuously assail the ear; the play of light, shade, and color discernible even through closed eyelids; the wafting of smells into the nostrils; the lingering of tastes on the palate. When going about your daily business, stop occasionally; let go of whatever worries, fantasies, or plans are preoccupying you and imbibe the rich sensuous immediacy of the moment: the call of a startled blackbird slicing through the bass rumble of a truck.

To meditate is not to empty the mind and gape at things in

a trancelike stupor. Nothing significant will ever be revealed by just staring blankly at an object long and hard enough. To meditate is to probe with intense sensitivity each glimmer of color, each cadence of sound, each touch of another's hand, each fumbling word that tries to utter what cannnot be said.

The stiller the mind, the more palpable the dazzling torrent of life becomes. From the bubbling of thoughts to the collapse of empires, this changing world moves inexorably on, driven by conditions, diverted by choices, stunned by accidents. By focusing on each detail of experience with the same scrutiny, awareness discloses how I too am part of this, that there is nothing within it that I can rely on, nothing I can hold on to as "me" or "mine."

I OPEN THE refrigerator. The interior of the cold humming box reveals brightly labeled jars, saucers covered with foil, anonymous plastic bags, a perspiring can of chilled beer, illuminated in a way that reminds me of prisons. I cast my eye to where the milk should be but there is none, recalling in that moment how I used it up yesterday afternoon for coffee when S came around. The fridge door closes with the sound of a faint gasp, and the bowl on which I had fixed my attention as S spoke flashes before me. I swivel around on my right heel, catching as I do a blur of kitchen until my gaze settles first on the empty hook by the dog's leash and then on the keys still lying on the sideboard where I tossed them yesterday in fatigue and mild irritation. With the worn glint of key-metal the same irritation flickers from my solar plexus and lodges in my throat. I cough, pretending to myself that this might be the first symptom of a cold, and reach for the scarf lying over the back of a chair, then the coat hanging for once where it should be, on the stand by the door. I pull the door, but it's locked, and a muscle in my shoulder objects. I cross the room for the keys, almost tripping as I do but conceiving the motion as a dance step and for a second myself as Nureyev until my fingers touch the keys and I remember the rouged face of a man denying his own death. Sadly I enter the key into the lock, where it slips with reassuring ease, and I pull open the door to enter yet another world.

# BECOMING

*Confusion conditions activity, which conditions consciousness, which conditions embodied personality, which conditions sensory experience, which conditions impact, which conditions mood, which conditions craving, which conditions clinging, which conditions becoming, which conditions birth, which conditions aging and death.*

—The Buddha

### Confusion . . .

I AM CONFUSED. I am confused by the sheer irrationality, ambiguity, and abundance of things coming into being at all. I am confused by having been born into a world from which I will be ejected at death. I am confused as to who or why I am. I am confused by the labyrinth of choices I face. I don't know what to do.

This confusion is not a state of darkness in which I fail to see anything. It is partial blindness rather than sightlessness.

By not seeing well, I misconstrue things: like entering the pottery shed in the yard to discover a snake in one corner. My heart accelerates and I am frozen with fear. Only when my eyes get used to the light do I realize it is a coil of hose.

Might a similar confusion color my experience of life as a whole: a confusion that not only blinds me to what is happening but at the same time anxiously construes a fictional world that seems utterly real? I have a strange sense of inhabiting a reality in which I do not quite seem to fit. I suspect that I keep getting tangled up in things not because I fail to see them but because I imagine myself to be configured other than I am. I think of myself as a round peg trying to fit into a round hole, while unaware that I have become a square peg.

❧

*Confusion conditions activity, which conditions conscious-*
*ness, which conditions embodied personality . . .*

WHEN YOU FIRST try to make a pot on a wheel, the clay does not obey your fingers. You end up with a wet, muddy mess. With practice, though, you become adept at handling clay in relation to the spin of the wheel and can create functional and beautiful things. I likewise have become adept at configuring myself from the spinning clay of my existence, creating a personality, a home, friendships, children, ideas.

If only the endeavor were not disfigured by confusion and turmoil. Frustration and bitterness grow instead of compassion and understanding. I silently rage at a world that fails to appreciate me. I want just to be left in peace, to be loved and accepted, but for some reason people either ignore me or dismiss me. Becoming maudlin and self-pitying only makes things worse, but I can't help it.

So I set out on the absurd task of reordering the world to fit my agenda. I try to create a perfect situation, one in which I have everything I want and nothing I don't want. I dream of a life in which all imperfections are removed. In doing so I find myself at odds with the very presence of things.

I find myself confronted with the stubbornness of matter, the fickleness of mood, the ambiguity of perception, the wilfulness of thought and habit. As a way of controlling these I split reality into two parts: the bit that is mine and the bit that is not. My body stands in opposition not only to your body but to all other matter. My feelings are the only ones that really count. My version of events is always right. The imperative of my craving is set against the imperative of yours.

I do not experience matter, mood, perception, and impulse as such but as unique chaotic moments configured in unprecedented and unrepeatable ways. This complex specificity becomes present because I *name* what I experience. Do I ever perceive a dangerous arrangement of shapes and colors? No. *There's a snake in the pottery shed!*

This is nowhere more evident than with an embodied personality. And it is all summed up in a name. Whether someone calls out my name or I see it on an envelope, it captures me as vividly as does a mirror image or a photograph. "Yes, that's me," I think. Just as I would look across the street and say, "Oh! There's S."

When the division between myself and the rest of the world is driven by confusion and turmoil, this sharp differentiation hardens even further. My distinctiveness is frozen into an absolute aloneness. I feel abandoned, trapped in my body.

Again, I need to stop. I may be able to start thawing this isolation by focusing on the complexity that I am. I may be able to ease the spasm of self-centeredness by realizing that I am not a fixed essence but an interactive cluster of processes.

SIT STILL AND come back to the breath. Center your attention in the rhythm of sensations that make up the act of breathing. Let the agitated mind settle, then expand your awareness to include the rest of the body. With calm alertness gradually increase the field of awareness until you encompass the totality of your experience in this moment: what you hear, see, smell, taste, and touch, as well as the thoughts and emotions that arise and fade in your mind.

Notice how your senses are flooded by a ceaseless stream of colors, shapes, sounds, smells, tastes, textures, and ideas. The moving world flies toward this sensitive instrument from all directions. As soon as it makes contact, it resonates inside you with an ineffable but distinctive tone. The experience of the world is colored with a rich range of feelings and moods which we cannot help having. Each experience registers somewhere along a spectrum between ecstasy and agony. Pay attention to this tonal quality, observing how it permeates both body and mind—but is singularly difficult to pin down.

Notice also, despite its diversity and complexity, how the world is always present in a way that makes sense. Even when you hear a birdsong you don't recognize, you make sense of it by noting to yourself: "I don't know that one." If a person blind from birth were suddenly able to see, he would not open his eyes and just behold the world of the sighted. He would behold a bewildering array of colors and shapes, which he then would learn to make sense of. The world is so saturated with the meanings given to it that those meanings seem to reside in the things themselves. We habitually assume the world presented through the senses to exist out there just as it appears. It really seems, for example, as though these black squiggles on a white ground are saying something about the nature of perception. As you listen to sounds and observe sensations in the body, consider how what you experience is configured by your own conditioning, habits, and views.

Notice too how the world is always an arena of possibilities. When you are sitting, you face the possibilities of standing, walking, or lying down. When you are silent, you face the possibility of speech. At every moment we are either inclining toward or engaged in an act: a physical movement, an utterance, a thought. Even when you decide not to act, you are still doing something: refraining. Notice how even when the mind is quiet it is still tensed, ready to spring into action.

The mere fact that life is always open to possibilities enables you to have a sense of purpose and direction. The intentions that arise in the privacy of your thoughts can subsequently be realized in the world. As you sit in meditation, notice how what you are doing is the enactment of an earlier resolve. By attending to the details of this present moment, by choosing not to recollect the past or plan for the future, you are engaged in a process of *creating* yourself in a specific and deliberate way.

But what is this self that you create? Repeat your name or say to yourself "I" or "me." What image or feeling does this evoke? Does the self exist in the body, the mind, or both? Or somewhere apart from them? If you search for it, what do you find?

If the self feels like a physical sensation, then probe that sensation to find what it is. If it feels like a mood, a perception, a volition, then probe them too. The closer you look, the more you might discover how every candidate for self dissolves into something else. Instead of a fixed nugget of "me," you find yourself experiencing a medley of sensations, moods, perceptions, and intentions, working together like the crew of a boat, steered by the skipper of attention.

But how easily this vision of fluctuating, interactive processes switches back into the habitual image of an isolated ego. How natural it seems for confusion to burst in again and for the drudgery of an anguished existence to resume.

＞

*... embodied personality conditions sensory experience,
which conditions impact, which conditions mood ...*

I AM LOST in preoccupation with myself, my fears, my longings, my memories, my plans. Whether walking, standing, sitting, or lying down, I am trapped in the prison of my own inner obsessions. I peer out on the world as though upon a foreign land.

The speed at which the world impacts upon my senses, together with my habit of treating it as either an ally or a threat, leads to confusion about the origin of my moods. If I find a piece of music unpleasant, I tend to blame the jarring notes for my discomfort (even while someone beside me enjoys it). When there is no obvious reason for feeling gloomy, I cast about for someone or something to blame and tend to come up with a culprit (a sleepless night, S, new shoes). The same is true with pleasure—even though I know that a kiss prolonged beyond a certain point turns into slobbery drool and a crick in the neck.

Impact and mood trigger my habitual patterns of perception and reaction. Just as rainfall runs along the gutters and drains designed to catch it, so my interaction with the world tends to follow the most familiar and least resistant course. When I see the snake in the shed, everything I have ever known or feared about snakes configures my sense of the world at that moment. And as I stand there frozen in terror, possible actions flash before me: do I rush for the door? tiptoe out slowly? scare it away? kill it?

But these seemingly irresistible feelings, perceptions, and impulses are not the only options. For in the immediacy of that experience lies the freedom to see more clearly. I can stop, pay attention to the breath, feel my beating heart, and remember to be aware. Then I may respond with care and intelligence to the snake's presence. Or realize it is just a coil of hose.

➤

*. . . mood conditions craving, which conditions clinging,*
*which conditions becoming . . .*

MOODS DICTATE MY behavior. If something makes me feel good, I want to have it; if it makes me feel bad, I want to get rid of it; if it leaves me indifferent, I ignore it. I find myself in a perpetual state of conflict: emotionally pulled one way and pushed the other. Yet underpinning both attraction and aversion is craving: the childish and utopian thirst for a situation in which I finally possess everything I desire and have repelled everything I dislike. Deep down I insist that a permanent, separate self is entitled to a life removed from the contingencies and uncertainties of existence.

And I invest my icons of craving with absolute finality. Be they sex, fame, or wealth, they shine before me with an intoxicating allure unsullied by the ambiguities of lived experience. I do not consider their implications. Diapers and tantrums figure as little in my fantasies of sexual conquest as do journalists and taxes in my daydreams of fame and wealth.

Such craving is crystallized from the spinning turmoil of confusion. In my metaphorical blindness, I reach out desperately for something to cling to. I yearn for anything that might assuage the sense of loss, anguish, isolation, aimlessness. But craving is distorted and disturbed by the very confusion it seeks to dispel. It exaggerates the desirability of what it longs to possess and the hatefulness of what it wants to be rid of. Bewitched by its own projections, it elevates its goals into matters of supreme significance. Under the spell of craving, my whole life hinges on the acquisition or banishment of something. "If only . . ." becomes the mantra of unconsummated desire.

A world of contingency and change can offer only simulacra of perfection. When driven by craving, I am convinced that if only I were to achieve *this* goal, all would be well. While creating the illusion of a purposeful life, craving is really the loss of direction. It is a process of compulsive becoming. It spins me around in circles, covering the same ground again and again. Each time I think I have found a situation that solves all my problems, it suddenly turns out to be a reconfiguration of the very situation I thought I was escaping from. My sense of having found a new lease on life turns out to be merely a repetition of the past. I realize I am running on the spot, frantically going nowhere.

&gt;

*. . . becoming conditions birth, which conditions aging
and death.*

LIFE BECOMES A succession of minibirths and minideaths. When I achieve what I want, I feel reborn. But no sooner have I settled into this feeling than the old anxieties resurface. The new possession swiftly ages as it is diminished by the allure of something more desirable that I do not have. What seemed perfect is abruptly compromised by alarming glimpses of its imperfections. Instead of solving my problems, this new situation replaces them with others I had never suspected. Yet rather than accepting this as the nature of living in an unreliable world, rather than learning to be content with success and joy and not to be overwhelmed by failure and pain, rather than appreciating life's poignant, tragic, and sad beauty, I grit my teeth and struggle on in thrall to that quiet, seductive voice that whispers: "If only . . ."

# EMPTINESS

*Unborn emptiness has let go of the extremes of being and non-being. Thus it is both the center itself and the central path. Emptiness is the track on which the centered person moves.*

— Tsongkhapa

PICK UP A ballpoint pen. Take off the cap and ask: "Is this still a ballpoint pen?" Yes, of course—albeit one without a cap. Unscrew the top part of the casing, remove the ink refill, and screw the top on again. Is that a ballpoint pen? Well, yes, just about. Is the refill a ballpoint pen? No, it's just the refill—but at least it can function as a pen, unlike the empty casing. Take the two halves of the casing apart. Is either of them a ballpoint pen? No, definitely not. No way.

What happens to the thing as you dismantle it? When do

the components cease (or start) to become a pen? When does the banana you are eating stop being a banana? When does the lump of clay on the wheel start being a pot? Names and concepts suggest there are objects in the world every bit as definite as themselves. Pens, bananas, and pots are self-evident, instantly recognizable things. But subject them to a little scrutiny, and that certainty begins to waver. Things are not as clear-cut as they seem. They are neither circumscribed nor separated from each other by lines. Lines are drawn in the mind. There are no lines in nature.

Sit on a chair, close your eyes, and listen attentively to the rain falling outside. Where does the sound of the rain stop and your hearing of it begin? Where, for that matter, does your bottom end and the seat of the chair begin? While conceptually the sound of rain is as different from my hearing as my bottom is from the chair, experientially it is impossible to distinguish between them. Rainfall blurs into hearing; bottom blurs into chair.

Consider the bulb of a daffodil buried in the ground all winter. As the weather gets warmer, it begins to sprout. If it rains sufficiently, there is no frost, and no one treads on it, one morning you will exclaim: "Look! The daffodils are out." But did the sprout suddenly cease to be a sprout and in its place a daffodil appear? The same problem: while a sprout is no more a daffodil than a daffodil is a sprout, somehow the sprout becomes a daffodil. The dividing line between sprout and daffodil is a convenient conceptual and linguistic distinction that cannot be found in nature.

In this sense, ballpoint pens, bananas, pots, rainfall, hearing, chairs, bottoms, sprouts, and daffodils have no beginning and no end. They neither start nor do they stop. They neither are born nor do they die. They emerge from a matrix of conditions and in turn become part of another matrix of conditions from which something else emerges.

IN EVERYDAY EXPERIENCE, one thing leads to the next. I become irritated by something S said to me and end up wanting to hit him. I imagine I see a snake in the pottery shed and freeze in terror. Everything that happens emerges out of what preceded it. Everything we do now becomes a condition for what is possible later.

We may speak of conditions and consequences as though they were things, but if we look more closely they turn out to be processes with no independent reality. The harshness of a barbed remark that haunts us for days is no more than a brief instance isolated from a torrent of events. Yet it stands out in the mind's eye as something intrinsically real and apart. This habit of isolating things leads us to inhabit a world in which the gaps between them become absolute. The snake in the shed is really there, as sharply differentiated from the frightened person who beholds it as from the shards of discarded pottery on which it is coiled.

Clutching at ourselves and the world in this way is a precondition for anguish. By regarding things as absolutely separate and as desirable or fearful in themselves, we set ourselves the task of possessing something we can never have or of eradicating something that was never there in the first place. Noticing how things emerge from and fade back into an unbroken flow of conditions begins to free us a little. We recognize how things are relatively, not absolutely, desirable or fearful. They interconnect and interact, each contingent on the others, no one of them intrinsically separate from the rest.

Whatever emerges in this way is devoid of an intrinsic identity: in other words, things are empty. They are not as opaque and solid as they seem: they are transparent and fluid. They are not as singular and straightforward as they seem:

they are complex and ambiguous. They are not only defined by philosophy, science, and religion: they are evoked through the play of allusions, paradoxes, and jokes. They cannot be pinned down with certainty: they trigger perplexity, amazement, and doubt.

❧

THE SAME IS true for each one of us. Just as a potter forms a pot on the wheel, so I configure my personality from the spinning clay of my existence. The pot does not exist in its own right: it emerges from the interactions of the potter, the wheel, the clay, its shape, its function (each of which in·turn emerges from the interactions of its causes and components ad infinitum). There is no essential pot to which its attributes adhere—just as there is no essential daffodil to which stalk, leaves, petals, and stamen adhere. Pots and daffodils are configurations of causes, conditions, parts, functions, language, images. They are devoid of an identity stamped like a serial number in the core of their being.

And so is each of us. As a human being I am more complex than a pot or a daffodil, but I have also emerged from causes and am composed of diverse, changing features and traits. There is no essential me that exists apart from this unique configuration of biological and cultural processes. Even if intellectually I agree with this, intuitively it may not be how I feel about myself. In any event, dharma practice is concerned not with proving or disproving theories of self but with understanding and easing the grip of self-centeredness that constricts body, feelings, and emotions into a tight nugget of anguish.

Imagine you are at a crowded exhibition of Ming porcelain. A voice calls out: "Hey! Thief! Stop!" Everyone in the room turns to look at you. Although you haven't stolen anything, the glare of accusation and disapproval provokes intense self-consciousness. You stand as exposed as though you were naked. You—or rather the tight nugget of anguish—blurts out: "It wasn't me! *Honest*."

It is as though this self—which is a mere configuration of past and present contingencies—has been fired in the kiln of anxiety to emerge as something fixed. Fixed but also brittle. The more precious it becomes to me, the more I must guard it against attack. The circumstances in which I feel at ease become ever narrower and more circumscribed.

SELF-CONSCIOUSNESS IS AT once the most obvious and central fact of my life and the most elusive. If I search for my self in meditation, I find it is like trying to catch my own shadow. I reach for it, but there's nothing there. Then it reappears elsewhere. I glimpse it from the corner of my mind's eye, turn to face it, and it's gone. Each time I think I've pinned it down, it turns out to be something else: a bodily sensation, a mood, a perception, an impulse, or simply awareness itself.

I cannot find the self by pointing my finger at any physical or mental trait and saying: "Yes, that's me." For such traits come and go, whereas the sense of "I" remains constant. But neither can I put my finger on something other than these traits that—however ephemeral and contingent they may be—nonetheless define me.

The self may not be something, but neither is it nothing. It is simply ungraspable, unfindable. I am who I am not because of an essential self hidden away in the core of my being but because of the unprecedented and unrepeatable matrix of conditions that have formed me. The more I delve into this mystery of who I am (or what anything is), the more I just keep going. There is no end to it, only an infinite trajectory that avoids falling into the extremes of being and nonbeing.

This trajectory is not only the center, which is free from this duality, but the central path itself.

―

"EMPTINESS," SAID THE Tibetan philosopher Tsong-khapa, in 1397, "is the track on which the centered person moves." The word he uses for track is *shul*. This term is defined as "an impression": a mark that remains after that which made it has passed by—a footprint, for example. In other contexts, *shul* is used to describe the scarred hollow in the ground where a house once stood, the channel worn through rock where a river runs in flood, the indentation in the grass where an animal slept last night. All these are *shul:* the impression of something that used to be there.

A path is a *shul* because it is an impression in the ground left by the regular tread of feet, which has kept it clear of obstructions and maintained it for the use of others. As a *shul,* emptiness can be compared to the impression of something that used to be there. In this case, such an impression is formed by the indentations, hollows, marks, and scars left by the turbulence of selfish craving. When the turmoil subsides, we experience tranquillity, relief, and freedom.

To know emptiness is not just to understand the concept. It is more like stumbling into a clearing in the forest, where suddenly you can move freely and see clearly. To experience emptiness is to experience the shocking absence of what normally determines the sense of who you are and the kind of reality you inhabit. It may last only a moment before the habits of a lifetime reassert themselves and close in once more. But for that moment, we witness ourselves and the world as open and vulnerable.

This calm, free, open, and sensitive space is the very center of dharma practice. It is immediate, imminent, and dynamic. It is a path, a track. It grants an intimation of the invisible point to which the lines of our life converge. It allows unobstructed movement. And it assures us that we are not alone: it implies indebtedness to those who have trodden this path before and responsibility to those who will follow.

❧

"EMPTINESS" IS A confusing term. Although used as an abstract noun, it does not in any way denote an abstract thing or state. It is not something we "realize" in a moment of mystical insight that "breaks through" to a transcendent reality concealed behind yet mysteriously underpinning the empirical world. Nor do things "arise" from emptiness and "dissolve" back into it as though it were some kind of formless, cosmic stuff. These are just some of the ways emptiness has been appropriated as a metaphor of metaphysical and religious consolation.

"Emptiness" is a starkly unappetizing term used to undercut yearnings for such consolation. Yet ironically it has been called into the service of such longings. *Shunyata* (emptiness) is rendered into English as "the Void" by translators who overlook the fact that the term is neither prefixed by a definite article ("the") nor exalted with a capital letter, both of which are absent in classical Asian languages. From here it is only a hop, skip, and a jump to equating emptiness with such metaphysical notions as "the Absolute," "the Truth," or even "God." The notion of emptiness falls prey to the very habit of mind it was intended to undermine.

❧

EMPTINESS IS AS devoid of intrinsic being as a pot, a banana, or a daffodil. And if there were no pots, bananas, or daffodils, there would be no emptiness either. Emptiness does not deny that such things exist; it merely describes how they are devoid of an intrinsic, separate being. Emptiness is not apart from the world of everyday experience; it only makes sense in the context of making pots, eating bananas, and growing daffodils. A life centered in awareness of emptiness is simply an appropriate way of being in this changing, shocking, painful, joyous, frustrating, awesome, stubborn, and ambiguous reality. Emptiness is the central path that leads not beyond this reality but right into its heart. It is the track on which the centered person *moves*.

And we too are impressions left by something that used to be here. We have been created, molded, formed by a bewildering matrix of contingencies that have preceded us. From the patterning of the DNA derived from our parents to the firing of the hundred billion neurons in our brains to the cultural and historical conditioning of the twentieth century to the education and upbringing given us to all the experiences we have ever had and choices we have ever made: these have conspired to configure the unique trajectory that culminates in this present moment. What is here now is the unrepeatable impression left by all of this, which we call "me." Yet so vivid and startling is this image that we confuse what is a mere impression for something that exists independently of what formed it.

So what are we but the story we keep repeating, editing, censoring, and embellishing in our heads? The self is not like the hero of a B-movie, who remains unaffected by the storms of passion and intrigue that swirl around him from the opening credits to the end. The self is more akin to the complex and ambiguous characters who emerge, develop, and suffer across the pages of a novel. There is nothing thinglike about me at all. I am more like an unfolding narrative.

As we become aware of all this, we can begin to assume greater responsibility for the course of our lives. Instead of clinging to habitual behavior and routines as a means to secure this sense of self, we realize the freedom to create who we are. Instead of being bewitched by impressions, we start to create them. Instead of taking ourselves so seriously, we discover the playful irony of a story that has never been told in quite this way before.

# COMPASSION

*Even when I do things for the sake of others*
*No sense of amazement or conceit arises.*
*It is just like feeding myself;*
*I hope for nothing in return.*

—Shantideva

IMAGINE THREE PEOPLE sitting in front of you: a
friend, an enemy, and a stranger. (Don't worry about the
details, just feel their presence as though they were there but
your eyes were shut.) Settle the mind on the breath, then
consider each person in turn, noticing how the image you
have of them provokes a certain mood. Just as the friend
makes you feel relaxed and secure, the enemy (or someone
like S) makes you uncomfortable and nervous, while the
stranger (the woman at the supermarket checkout) evokes
only courteous disinterest.

What is it about them that makes you feel this way? A single incident, perhaps—something they said or did to you, the way they looked at you once—becomes a defining moment in which you freeze an image of them like a snapshot. With those you know well, this image is continuously edited and updated; with those you merely admire or disdain from a distance or with those who mean nothing to you, a brief encounter can confine them forever in an image that only becomes more intransigent with time. In each case, your impression of the other person is based upon how they have made you feel: you like those who make you feel good, dislike those who don't, and care little for anyone else.

Stay for a while with these images and their corresponding feelings. Notice how the way you perceive people reinforces your feelings about them, and how the way you feel about them reinforces your perceptions of them. The image we have of another becomes a confused mix of objective facts (long nose, wears glasses, balding) and our own ideas about him (arrogant, stupid, doesn't like me anymore). So as well as being someone in his own right, the person is cast as an actor in our own private psychodrama. It becomes increasingly hard to disentangle him from the emotionally charged image formed by our own desires and fears.

To escape this trap is not to pretend to feel otherwise but to start looking at things differently. We are free to choose how to perceive the world. Upon reflection, we may discover that no matter how strongly we feel about a person, that feeling is often based entirely on an image we have formed of him. Such is the nature of prejudice: because of a person's skin color, nationality, religion, etc., we immediately feel a certain way about him. This kind of meditation directly challenges the fixed images we have of others. By suspending our judgments, we are able to look at the person from a fresh perspective.

Start with the friend. Imagine her as a newborn baby,

covered in blood. Slowly follow her as she grows from a toddler to a child to an adolescent to a young adult to the moment you first met her. Try to picture what her hopes and longings were before she even suspected your existence. Think of her now as someone who values her own ideas and feelings in the same inscrutable way you hold on to yours. Then look into the future and watch her age, fall ill, grow old, and die.

Turn to the enemy and stranger and do the same, until three human beings sit before you: equal in birth and equal in death.

Does this perspective affect the way you feel about each person? Are you able, even for a moment, to witness these people in all their autonomy, mystery, majesty, tragedy? Can you see them as ends in their own right rather than means to your ends? Can you notice the restrictive and selective nature of the image you have formed of them? Can you let go of the craving to embrace the friend and banish the enemy? Can you love the stranger?

~

IF I TRIP and bang my knee on the sidewalk, my hand instinctively reaches out to soothe the pain. I sit down and tenderly massage it. I inspect the damage, then get up and walk home to treat it, being careful not to exacerbate the injury by putting too much weight on that leg. Yet only the knee is in pain. The hand has not been hurt, nor has the eye that studies the grazed, bruised skin, nor the other leg, which assumes the burden of the weakened knee.

When my friend appears at the door and greets me with a smile and a hug, I know she is in distress just by the flicker of her eyelids and the catch in her voice as she says "Hi!" In that moment her anguish pierces me and I sense it is because of something S has said or done to her. I become an intimate participant in her anguish as she recounts what happened. Yet I did not suffer the pain he caused her.

At such times compassion is natural and unhesitating: I respond to the suffering of my friend just as my hand or eye responds to my throbbing knee. But when I come across a down-and-out huddled in an alley, I may feel only a twinge of embarrassment or pity before tossing him a coin and hurrying on my way. Or if I am told that S has suffered a setback I may be secretly glad even as I hear myself saying how sorry I feel for the guy.

My compassion readily extends to those on one side of the invisible barrier that segregates me from the rest of the world. My knee, my friends, my family, my community, my colleagues—all belong to the domain of "me" and "mine." The bonds that unite us, be they common parents or an arbitrary preference for the same football team, are exaggerated by desire for belonging and fear of rejection. This in turn leads to a hardening perception of "us" and "them." In erecting this invisible barrier, perception again determines my mood: I feel good about "us," bad or indifferent toward "them."

But it is not always like this. There are times when the barrier is lifted. I find myself moved by the plight of those I do not know and probably never will: the hungry child, the abandoned dog, the streams of refugees. Or my world is suddenly transfigured by the smile of an old woman on a park bench. And when I finally run into S and he tells me how scared he's been of telling anyone he's HIV positive, all the resentment vanishes and his grief and terror become mine too.

For as long as these fragile moments last, I inhabit a world where all living things are united by their yearning to survive and be unharmed. I recognize the anguish of others not as theirs but as ours. It is as though the whole of life has been revealed as a single organism: reaching out to someone in pain is as natural and unself-conscious as my hand's reaching out to my injured knee.

While in the grip of self-centeredness, compassion remains restricted to those we feel to be on our side. The strength of this hold cannot be underestimated. It is like a spasm that seizes body, emotions, and soul. Yet so familiar is it that we either fail to notice it or regard it as "normal." When its grasp is loosened through the look in an old woman's eyes, the world is transfigured, and we know what it means for the heart to open. Even the momentary experience of a nonself-centered perspective on life is accompanied by affective expansion, exhilaration, and warmth—as though the spasm has let go.

Dharma practice is the cultivation of a way of life in which such moments are not just left to chance. However much we may treasure and value these moments, we soon find ourselves swept along again on the tides of unreflective self-absorption. But there is another choice: we can continually question the assumption of a fixed, immutable nugget of self at the core of experience. And we can persistently challenge the validity of the emotionally charged images by which we define others. Through both disciplined meditation and ongoing reflective inquiry, we can loosen the grip in which habitual perceptions of self and others hold us.

INSIGHT INTO EMPTINESS and compassion for the world are two sides of the same coin. To experience ourselves and the world as interactive processes rather than aggregates of discrete things undermines both habitual ways of perceiving the world as well as habitual feelings about it. Meditative discipline is vital to dharma practice precisely because it leads us beyond the realm of ideas to that of felt-experience. Understanding the philosophy of emptiness is not enough. The ideas need to be translated through meditation into the word-less language of feeling in order to loosen those emotional knots that keep us locked in a spasm of self-preoccupation.

As we are released into the opening left by the absence of self-centered craving, we experience the vulnerability of ex-posure to the anguish and suffering of the world. The track on which we find ourselves in moments of centered experi-ence includes both clarity of mind and warmth of heart. Just as a lamp simultaneously generates light and heat, so the central path is illuminated by wisdom and nurtured by com-passion.

The selfless vulnerability of compassion requires the vig-ilant protection of mindful awareness. It is not enough to *want* to feel this way toward others. We need to be alert at all times to the invasion of thoughts and emotions that threaten to break in and steal this open and caring resolve. A compas-sionate heart still feels anger, greed, jealousy, and other such emotions. But it accepts them for what they are with equa-nimity, and cultivates the strength of mind to let them arise and pass without identifying with or acting upon them.

Compassion is not devoid of discernment and courage. Just as we need the courage to respond to the anguish of others, so we need the discernment to know our limitations and the ability to say "no." A compassionate life is one in which our resources are used to optimum effect. Just as we need to know when and how to give ourselves fully to a task, so we need to know when and how to stop and rest.

◆

THE GREATEST THREAT to compassion is the temptation to succumb to fantasies of moral superiority. Exhilarated by the outpouring of selfless altruism toward others, we may come to believe that we are their savior. We find ourself humbly assuming the identity of one who has been singled out by destiny to heal the sorrows of the world and show the way to reconciliation, peace, and Enlightenment. Our words of advice to those in distress imperceptibly change into exhortations to humanity. Our suggestions of a course of action for a friend are converted into a moral crusade.

When subverted in this way, compassion exposes us to the danger of messianic and narcissistic inflation. Exaggerated rejection of self-centeredness can detach us from the sanity of ironic self-regard. Once inflation has taken hold—particularly when endorsed by supporters and admirers—it becomes notoriously difficult to see through it.

COMPASSION IS THE very heart and soul of awakening. While meditation and reflection can make us more receptive to it, it cannot be contrived or manufactured. When it erupts within us, it feels as though we have stumbled across it by chance. And it can vanish just as suddenly as it appeared. It is glimpsed in those moments when the barrier of self is lifted and individual existence is surrendered to the well-being of existence as a whole. It becomes abundantly clear that we cannot attain awakening for ourselves: we can only participate in the awakening of life.

# FRUITION

*The way of the Buddha is to know yourself;*

*To know yourself is to forget yourself;*

*To forget yourself is to be awakened by all things.*

— Dogen

*Genjo Koan*

# FREEDOM

*Therefore we know that, unawakened, even a Buddha is a sentient being, and that even a sentient being, if he is awakened in an instant of thought, is a Buddha.*

—Hui Neng

WHEN A MAN is released from a prison, he recovers his freedom. The moment he steps outside the gate, he is freed from his sentence, the wardens, the walls, bars, and locks of his cell. The world lies open before him; he is free to realize the possibilities it now offers. And he is free for others: available for relationships, available for whatever demands and challenges others present him.

Freedom is never absolute; it is always relative to something else: freedom *from* constraints, freedom *to* act, freedom *for* others. The former prisoner is still constrained by the laws of society, the resources available to him, the limits of his culture, knowledge, and skills, and ultimately the state of his body and the laws of nature.

Similarly, the freedom of awakening is a relative freedom *from* the constraints of self-centered confusion and turmoil, *from* the craving for a fixed identity, *from* the compulsion to contrive a perfect situation, *from* identification with preconceived opinions, and *from* the anguish that originates in such attachments. The Buddha himself was still constrained by the worldview of his time; his own language, knowledge, and skills; his awareness of what his society would tolerate; the availability of resources and technologies; the geographical and political barriers that restricted him to a limited area of northern India; his physical body, and the laws of nature.

Yet the world lay open to him in an unprecedented way. He was free *to* creatively realize its possibilities unhindered by the cravings that had previously determined his choices, free *to* imagine an appropriate response to the anguish of others, free *to* cultivate an authentic path that embraced all aspects of human life, free *to* form a community of friendships, and free *to* create a culture of awakening that would survive long after his death.

And he was free *for* others. He altruistically surrendered his personal well-being for their sake. He made himself available for whatever demands and challenges others presented him.

THE FREEDOM OF awakening is grounded in the cessation of craving. Such freedom is possible because the changing, contingent, ambiguous, and creative character of reality is *by its very nature* free.

We are are own jailers. We keep ourselves unfree by clinging, out of confusion and fear, to a self that exists independently of all conditions. Instead of accepting and understanding things as they are, we seek independence from them in the fiction of an isolated selfhood. Ironically, this alienated self-centeredness is then confused with individual freedom. The aim of dharma practice is to free ourselves from this illusion of freedom. This is achieved by understanding the anguish that accompanies such delusive independence, and letting go of the confusion and craving that hold it in place.

Cultivation of the path begins with an authentic vision of the changing, contingent, and creative character of ourself and the world. While initially the experience of reality's intrinsic freedom may be momentary and sporadic, dharma practice embraces a way of life that values this experience as normative rather than exceptional. Although we still may be overwhelmed by the turbulent patterns of habit, our commitment to this vision of freedom remains unwavering. To undermine the fixated, frozen view of things that traps us in cycles of craving and anguish, we need to cultivate awareness of the freedom present in each moment of experience.

➤

As LONG AS you are unmindful of the breath, it carries on in its own way. But as soon as you start paying attention to it, you tend to constrain it. Even if you tell yourself: "Just observe it as it is," the very act of self-conscious observation makes it stilted and controlled. You might have the sense that "I am breathing" rather than "it breathes."

Try this: at the end of the next out-breath, just *wait* for the following in-breath to occur—as though you were a cat waiting for a mouse to emerge from its hole. You know that the next in-breath will come, but you have no idea precisely when. So while your attention remains as alert and poised in the present as that of a cat's, it is free from any intention to control what will happen next. Without expectation, just wait. Then suddenly it happens and you catch "it" breathing.

It is strangely exhilarating (even unnerving) to be aware of the breath in this way. As a focus for mindfulness, the breath is the one bodily function that can be both autonomous and volitional (unlike, for example, the heartbeat). While the breath may initially serve as an object of concentration, by letting go of any urge to control it we can witness in its rhythmic motions the intrinsic freedom of reality itself.

Breathing is the movement of life, the vital process that connects the body with its environment. The more we open and deepen awareness of the breath and the body, the more we understand the intrinsic dynamism of our entire experience. Nothing stands still for a moment. Breath, heartbeat, body, feelings, thoughts, environment are facets of an indivisible, interactive system, no part of which can really be claimed as "me" or "mine."

Why then do we compulsively hold ourselves aloof and apart from all this? What constrains and inhibits us from fully participating in this experience? We may know full well that such participation will not obliterate us; it is perfectly compatible with the sane detachment of ironic self-regard. Yet still we identify with this ghostly self, hovering above and eternally isolated from the very processes of life. As a result, the entire interactive system feels as though it is jammed. And we feel numb, blocked, frustrated, unfree.

Repeatedly embracing the dynamic, precarious, and selfless flow of experience gradually erodes this ingrained conviction of our separate existence. To enhance this further still, it helps to let go not just of attachment to a fixed self but of all views that confine and fix experience. This can be achieved by recognizing that however we describe it (even as "dynamic, precarious, and selfless"), what is happening is utterly mysterious.

AS MINDFUL AWARENESS becomes stiller and clearer, experience becomes not only more vivid but simultaneously more baffling. The more deeply we know something in this way, the more deeply we don't know it. As we attentively listen to the rain or look at a chair, these familiar things become not only more apparent but also more puzzling. As we sit there aware of the breath, it is on the one hand ordinary and obvious, but on the other a mystery that we breathe at all. Attending to this dimension of experience where descriptions and explanations fail challenges assumptions about how we know. Experience cannot be accounted for by simply confining it to a conceptual category. Its ultimate ambiguity is that it is simultaneously knowable *and* unknowable. No matter how well we may know something, to witness its intrinsic freedom impels the humble admission: "*I don't really know it.*"

Such unknowing is not the end of the track: the point beyond which thinking can proceed no further. This unknowing is the basis of deep agnosticism. When belief and opinion are suspended, the mind has nowhere to rest. We are free to begin a radically other kind of questioning.

This questioning is present within unknowing itself. As soon as awareness finds itself baffled and puzzled by rainfall, a chair, the breath, they present themselves as questions. Habitual assumptions and descriptions suddenly fail and we hear our stammering voices cry out: "What is this?" Or simply: "What?" or "Why?" Or perhaps no words at all, just "?"

The sheer presence of things is startling. They provoke awe, wonder, incomprehension, shock. Not just the mind but the entire organism feels perplexed. This can be unsettling. Awareness now can be derailed easily by flashes of speculative thought, spontaneous bursts of poetry, which, no matter how inspired and original, cast us back into the categorized and familiar world.

The task of dharma practice is to sustain this perplexity within the context of calm, clear, and centered awareness. Such perplexity is neither frustrated nor merely curious about a specific detail of experience. It is an intense, focused questioning into the totality of what is unfolding at any given moment. It is the engine that drives awareness into the heart of what is unknown.

The questioning that emerges from unknowing differs from conventional inquiry in that it has no interest in finding an answer. This questioning starts at the point where descriptions and explanations end. It has already let go of the constraints and limitations of conceptual categories. It recognizes that mysteries are not solved as though they were problems and then forgotten. The deeper we penetrate a mystery, the more mysterious it becomes.

This perplexed questioning is the central path itself. In refusing to be drawn into the answers of "yes" and "no," "it is this," and "it is not that," it lets go of the extremes of affirmation and negation, something and nothing. Like life itself, it just keeps going, free from the need to hold to any fixed positions—including those of Buddhism. It prevents the quality of awareness from becoming a passive, routinized stance, which may accord with a belief system but renders experience numb and opaque. Perplexity keeps awareness on its toes. It reveals experience as transparent, radiant, and unimpeded. Questioning is the track on which the centered person *moves*.

Fired with intensity, but free from turbulence and the compulsion for answers, questioning is content just to let things be. There is not even a hidden agenda at work behind the scenes. Expectations of goals and rewards (such as Enlightenment) are recognized for what they are: last-ditch attempts by the ghostly self to subvert the process to its own ends. The more we become conscious of the mysterious unfolding of life, the clearer it becomes that its purpose is not to fulfill the expectations of our ego. We can put into words only the question it poses. And then let go, listen, and wait.

REALITY IS INTRINSICALLY free because it is changing, uncertain, contingent, and empty. It is a dynamic play of relationships. Awakening to this reveals our own intrinsic freedom, for we too are by nature a dynamic play of relationships. An authentic vision of this freedom is the ground of individual freedom and creative autonomy. This experience, however, is something we *recover* at specific moments in time. As long as we are locked into the assumption that self and things are unchanging, unambiguous, absolute, opaque, and solid, we will remain correspondingly confined, alienated, numbed, frustrated, and unfree.

Yet in practice, life cannot be so neatly split into the dualities of "free" and "unfree," "awakened" and "unawakened." While such categories are clear-cut, life is ambiguous. Freedom can be both recovered *and* lost again.

Awakening is the recovery of that awesome freedom into which we were born but for which we have substituted the pseudo-independence of a separate self. No matter how much it frightens us, no matter how much we resist it, such freedom is right at hand. It may break into our lives at any time, whether we seek it or not, enabling us to glimpse a reality that is simultaneously more familiar and more elusive than anything we have ever known, in which we find ourselves both profoundly alone and profoundly connected to everything. Yet the force of habit is such that suddenly it is lost again and we are back to unambiguous normality.

Through counteracting this force of habit, dharma

practice has two objectives: to let go of self-centered craving so that our lives become gradually more awake; and to be receptive to the sudden eruption of awakening into our lives at any moment. Awakening is both a linear process of freedom that is cultivated over time *and* an ever present possibility of freedom. The central path is both a track with a beginning and an end *and* the formless potentiality at the very center of experience.

# IMAGINATION

*[A] talent for speaking differently, rather than for arguing well, is the chief instrument of cultural change.*

—Richard Rorty

To DWELL IN unknowing perplexity before the breath, the rain, a chair is much the same as dwelling in unknowing perplexity before an unformed lump of clay, a blank sheet of paper, an empty computer screen. In both cases we find ourselves hovering on the cusp between nothing and something, formlessness and form, inactivity and activity. We are poised in a still, vital alertness on the threshold of creation, waiting for something to emerge (the next in-breath or the first tentative shaping of the clay) that has never happened in quite that way before and will never happen in quite that way again.

And in both cases we tremble on that fine line between exhilaration and dread. A meditator can be simultaneously enraptured by the intrinsic freedom of reality and unnerved by the symmetry-breaking cascade of experience about to burst forth in the next moment. Potters or writers can be enthralled by the endless creative possibilities of each moment but paralyzed by their hesitation to realize even one of them. Just as the meditator flees to the safety of a consoling memory or fantasy, so the artist races out to get another cup of coffee.

We could decide simply to remain absorbed in the mysterious, unformed, free-play of reality. This would be the choice of the mystic who seeks to extinguish himself in God or Nirvana—analogous perhaps to the tendency among artists to obliterate themselves with alcohol or opiates. But if we value our participation in a shared reality in which it makes sense to make sense, then such self-abnegation would deny a central element of our humanity: the need to speak and act, to share our experience with others.

❧

FREEDOM ENTAILS RESPONSIBILITY. Freedom *from* self-centered craving is freedom *to* creatively realize the possibilities of the world *for* others. When understanding and compassion are two sides of the same coin, an authentic vision of the empty and contingent nature of things spontaneously seeks to reflect itself in concrete and vivid forms of life. Face to face with the world, we struggle to find concepts, images, ideas through which to express the awesome inexpressibility of reality in authentic speech and acts. This unformed vision strives for form through imagination.

As an experience of freedom, awakening does not provide us with a set of ready-made ideas or images—let alone philosophical or religious doctrines. By its very nature it is free from the constraints of preconceived ideas, images, and doctrines. It offers no answers, only the possibility of new beginnings. In expressing it we no more translate concealed esoteric knowledge into wise utterances than a writer transposes fully formed sentences hidden in his mind onto paper.

Ideas and words emerge through the very process of expressing them to an actual or implied audience. They might come as a surprise, a shock—even to the person who articulates them. They do not arrive fully formed any more than a daffodil arrives fully formed from a sprouting bulb. They arise from an unrepeatable matrix of contingencies: the authenticity of our own vision and compassion in that moment, the needs of others in a particular time and place, our skill in using available technical and cultural resources.

DHARMA PRACTICE IS more akin to artistic creation than technical problem solving. The technical dimension of dharma practice (such as training to be more mindful and focused) is comparable to the technical skills a potter must learn in order to become proficient in his craft. Both may require many years of discipline and hard work. Yet for both such expertise is only a means, not an end in itself. Just as technical proficiency in pottery is no guarantee of beautiful pots, so technical proficiency in meditation is no guarantee of a wise or compassionate response to anguish.

The art of dharma practice requires commitment, technical accomplishment, and imagination. As with all arts, we will fail to realize its full potential if any of these three is lacking. The raw material of dharma practice is ourself and our world, which are to be understood and transformed according to the vision and values of the dharma itself. This is not a process of self- or world-transcendence, but one of self- and world-*creation*.

The denial of "self" challenges only the notion of a static self independent of body and mind—not the ordinary sense of ourself as a person distinct from everyone else. This notion of a static self is the primary obstruction to the realization of our unique potential as an individual being. By dissolving this fiction through a centered vision of the transiency, ambiguity, and contingency of experience, we are freed to create ourself anew. The notion of the world as an alien reality composed of stubborn, discrete things is likewise the primary obstruction to world-creation. In dissolving this view through a vision of the world as a dynamic and interrelated whole of which we are an integral part, we are likewise freed to engage with the world afresh.

To realize such visions requires acts of imagination. No matter how deeply we understand the transient and empty nature of existence, how vividly we experience the intrinsic freedom of reality, how passionately we long to appease the anguish of others, if we cannot imagine forms of life that respond effectively to the situation at hand, we will be limited in what we can do. Instead of finding a voice that speaks to the unique contingencies of our own situation, we repeat the clichés and dogmas of other epochs. Instead of creatively participating in a contemporary culture of awakening, we confine ourself to preserving those cultures of a vanishing past.

Self-creation entails imagining ourself in other ways. Instead of thinking of ourself as a fixed nugget in a shifting current of mental and physical processes, we might consider ourself as a narrative that transforms these processes into an unfolding story. Life becomes less of a defensive stance to preserve an immutable self and more of an ongoing task to complete an unfinished tale. As a coherent narrative, our identity's integrity is maintained without having to assume an unmoving metaphysical center around which everything else turns. Grounded in awareness of transiency, ambiguity, and contingency, such a person values lightness of touch, flexibility and adaptability, a sense of humor and adventure, appreciation of other viewpoints, a celebration of difference.

❧

As soon as the imagination is activated in the process of awakening, we recover the aesthetic dimension of dharma practice. The cultivation of focused awareness, for example, cannot be adequately understood as a set of cognitive and affective transformations alone, because such awareness is also an experience of beauty.

As the turmoil of consciousness subsides and we come to rest in a heightened clarity of attention, the natural beauty of the world is vividly enhanced. We marvel at the exquisite tracery of a leaf, the play of light against the bark of a tree, the reflections and ripples in a puddle of water, the deliquescent radiance of a human eye. Our appreciation of the arts is also enriched: a phrase of music, a line of poetry, a dancing figure, a penciled sketch, a clay vase may speak to us with unprecedented poignancy and depth.

Great works of art in all cultures succeed in capturing within the constraints of their form both the pathos of anguish and a vision of its resolution. Take, for example, the languorous sentences of Proust or the haiku of Basho, the late quartets and sonatas of Beethoven, the tragicomic brushwork of Sengai or the daunting canvases of Rothko, the luminous self-portraits of Rembrandt and Hakuin. Such works achieve their resolution not through consoling or romantic images whereby anguish is transcended. They accept anguish without being overwhelmed by it. They reveal anguish as that which gives beauty its dignity and depth.

The four ennobling truths of the Buddha provide not only a paradigm of cognitive and affective freedom but a template for aesthetic vision. Any work of art that deepens our understanding of anguish, moves us to relax the constrictions of self-centered craving, reveals the dynamic play of emptiness and form, and inspires a way of life conducive to such ends bears the hallmarks of authentic beauty. And just as non-Buddhist works can have such an effect, so explicitly Buddhist works can fail to do so.

The same aesthetic vision inspires the imaginative tasks of self- and world-creation. The ennobling truths are not just challenges to act with wisdom and compassion but challenges to act with creativity and aesthetic awareness. Our words, our deeds, our very presence in the world, create and leave impressions in the minds of others just as a writer makes impressions with his pen on paper, the painter with his brush on canvas, the potter with his fingers in clay. The human world is like a vast musical instrument on which we simultaneously play our part while listening to the compositions of others. The creation of ourself in the image of awakening is not a subjective but an intersubjective process. We cannot choose *whether* to engage with the world, only *how* to. Our life is a story being continuously related to others through every detail of our being: facial expressions, body language, clothes, inflections of speech—whether we like it or not.

AFTER HIS AWAKENING, the Buddha spent several weeks hovering on the cusp between the rapture of freedom and, in his words, the "vexation" of engagement. Should he remain in the peaceful state of Nirvana or share with others what he had discovered? What decided him was the appearance of an idea (in the language of ancient India, a "god") that forced him to recognize the potential for awakening in others and his responsibility to act. As soon as his imagination was triggered, he relinquished the mystical option of transcendent absorption and moved to engage with the world.

Thus the Buddha set out on a path that started from a vision, was translated through ideas into words and actions, and gave rise to cultures of awakening that continue to inspire today. This development is analogous to the process of creativity, which likewise starts from an unformed vision and is translated through the imagination into cultural forms. The course of the Buddha's life offers a paradigm of human existence, which has been realized in diverse forms throughout Asia over the past two and a half thousand years.

The genius of the Buddha lay in his imagination. He succeeded in translating his vision not only into the language of his time but into terms sufficiently universal to inspire future generations in India and beyond. His ideas have survived in much the same way as great works of art. While we may find certain stylistic elements of his teaching alien, his central ideas speak to us in a way that goes beyond their reference to a particular time or place. But unlike ancient statues from Egypt or Gandhara, the wheel of dharma set in motion by the Buddha continued to turn after his death, generating ever new and startling cultures of awakening.

EACH TIME THE dharma moved into a different civilization or historical period, it faced a twofold challenge: to maintain its integrity as an internally coherent tradition, and to express its vision in a way that responded to the needs of the new situation. In order to make sense, it had to imagine itself in original and unexpected ways (compare the Pali discourses, a collection of Zen koans, and the *Tibetan Book of the Dead*). While this gradual process of transformation occurred over several generations, it was invariably crystallized through the genius of a single person or, at most, a handful of individuals.

The genius of these people lay also in their imagination: their capacity to express an authentic vision of the dharma in a way that responded creatively to the needs of their particular situations. They initiated distinctive cultures of awakening that generated original and abundant outpourings of philosophy, literature, and art. Yet these periods of cultural vitalization did not tend to last long. For while the founding figures were imaginative and creative, imagination and creativity were rarely qualities encouraged in the schools and orders they established. (The very terms "imagination" and "creativity" lack exact equivalents in classical Buddhist languages.) As their traditions grew into powerful religious institutions, the preservation of orthodoxy became the main priority.

While originating in acts of imagination, orthodoxies paradoxically seek to control the imagination as a means of maintaining their authority. The authenticity of a person's understanding is measured according to its conformity with the dogmas of the school. While such controls may provide a necessary safeguard against charlatanism and self-deception, they also can be used to suppress authentic attempts at creative innovation that might threaten the status quo. The imagination is anarchic and potentially subversive. The more hierarchic and authoritarian a religious institution, the more it will require that the creations of the imagination conform to its doctrines and aesthetic norms.

Yet by suppression of the imagination, the very life of dharma practice is cut off at its source. While religious orthodoxies may survive and even prosper for centuries, in the end they will ossify. When the world around them changes, they will lack the imaginative power to respond creatively to the challenges of the new situation.

# CULTURE

*There is nothing not practiced*
*By those inspired by the Buddha;*
*When skilled in living this way,*
*There is nothing without value.*

—Shantideva

As Buddhism encounters the contemporary world, it discovers a situation where creativity and imagination are central to individual and social freedom. While Buddhist traditions have consistently affirmed freedom *from* craving and anguish as the raison d'être of a culture of awakening, they have been less consistent in affirming the freedom *to* respond creatively to the anguish of the world. Both internally, through becoming religious orthodoxies, and externally, through identifying with autocratic and even totalitarian regimes, Buddhist traditions have inclined toward political conservatism. This has contributed, on the one hand, to a tendency to mysticism and, on the other, to the postponing of personal and social fulfillment until a future rebirth in a less corrupted world.

At the heart of Buddhism's encounter with the contemporary world is the convergence of two visions of freedom. The Buddha's freedom from craving and anguish is converging with the autonomous individual's freedom to realize his or her capacity for personal and social fulfillment.

In today's liberal democracies we are brought up to realize our potential as autonomous individuals. It is hard to envisage a time when so many people have enjoyed comparable freedoms. Yet the very exercise of these freedoms in the service of greed, aggression, and fear has led to breakdown of community, destruction of the environment, wasteful exploitation of resources, the perpetuation of tyrannies, injustices, and inequalities. Instead of creatively realizing their freedoms, many choose the unreflective conformism dictated by television, indulgence in mass-consumerism, or numbing their feelings of alienation and anguish with drugs. In theory, freedom may be held in high regard; in practice it is experienced as a dizzying loss of meaning and direction.

Part of the appeal of any religious orthodoxy lies in its preserving a secure, structured, and purposeful vision of life, which stands in stark opposition to the insecurity, disorder, and aimlessness of contemporary society. In offering such a refuge, traditional forms of Buddhism provide a solid basis for the ethical, meditative, and philosophical values conducive to awakening. Yet they tend to be wary of participating in a translation of this liberating vision into a culture of awakening that addresses the specific anguish of the contemporary world. Preservation of the known and tested is preferable to the agony of imagination, where we are forced to risk that hazardous leap into the dark.

THE BUDDHIST AND contemporary visions of freedom both support *and* critique each other. The Buddhist vision seeks to cultivate a path of individual and social practice that leads to a liberating experience of self and world. It cannot accept the notion that authentic freedom can be realized in a life driven by confused self-centered craving. The contemporary vision strives to create and maintain social and political structures that uphold the rights and optimize the creative possibilities of the individual. It cannot accept the notion that authentic freedom can be realized in a repressive and unjust society.

While it would be futile to try to describe the culture of awakening that might result from the encounter of these visions, two broad themes are beginning to emerge. These are the distinctively contemporary ways in which dharma practice is becoming *individuated,* on the one hand, and *socially engaged*, on the other.

The individuation of dharma practice occurs whenever priority is given to the resolution of a personal existential dilemma over the need to conform to the doctrines of a Buddhist orthodoxy. Individuation is a process of recovering personal authority through freeing ourselves from the constraints of collectively held belief systems. If training with a teacher of a certain school leads to a growing dependency on that tradition and a corresponding loss of personal autonomy, then that allegiance may have to be severed. At the same time, unprecedented exposure to a wide range of Buddhist traditions today makes it difficult to accept each school's unquestioned assumption of its own superiority. In valuing imagination and diversity, such an individuated vision would ultimately empower each practitioner to create his or her own distinctive track within the field of dharma practice.

The contemporary social engagement of dharma practice is rooted in awareness of how self-centered confusion and craving can no longer be adequately understood only as psychological drives that manifest themselves in subjective states of anguish. We find these drives embodied in the very economic, military, and political structures that influence the lives of the majority of people on earth. Harnessed to industrial technologies, the impact of these drives affects the quality of the environment; the availability of natural resources and employment; the kinds of political, social, and financial institutions that govern peoples' lives. Such a socially engaged vision of dharma practice recognizes that each practitioner is obliged by an ethics of empathy to respond to the anguish of a globalized, interdependent world.

Individuation and social engagement are not unique to the contemporary situation. Whenever a culture of awakening has been realized in the past, it has arisen through the original, imaginative vision of an individual and subsequently has been embodied in social structures compatible with the new situation. Modern democracy, science, and education have led to the role of the individual in society and the nature of social relations being radically different today from former times in Asia. Commensurably diverse processes of individuation and social engagement are needed for the realization of a contemporary culture of awakening.

The self-creation of individuation and the world-creation of social engagement cannot exist apart from each other. They are united within a common culture, which configures them in a meaningful and purposeful whole. At the same time, it is the creative tension between them that constantly forms and shapes this culture. Individuation and social engagement become the two poles of a culture of awakening.

CULTURE, ACCORDING TO the Chambers dictionary, is the "state of being cultivated." What is to be cultivated, according to the Buddha, is a path of authentic vision, ideas, speech, action, forms of life, resolve, mindfulness, and focused awareness. Hence a culture of awakening is a state in which this path is being cultivated.

A culture of awakening is forged from the tension between an indebtedness to the past and a responsibility to the future. This tension is most palpable during transitional phases such as our own. To preserve the integrity of the tradition, we have to distinguish between what is central to that integrity and what is peripheral. We have to discern between what elements are vital for the survival of dharma practice and what are alien cultural artefacts that might obstruct that survival. A contemporary example is whether the metaphysical doctrines of karma and rebirth are integral to the tradition or not. Whatever decision we reach on such issues is a risk. We are obliged to assume responsibility for choices whose potentially considerable consequences for others we cannot possibly foresee.

A culture of awakening cannot exist independently of the specific social, religious, artistic, and ethnic cultures in which it is embedded. It emerges out of creative interactions with these cultures without either rejecting or being absorbed by them. It will inevitably assume certain features of contemporary culture, perhaps inspiring and revitalizing some dimensions of it, while also maintaining a critical perspective.

Dharma practice today faces two primary dangers: through resisting creative interaction, it could end up as a marginalized subculture, a beautifully preserved relic, while through losing its inner integrity and critical edge, it could end up being swallowed by something else, such as psycho-therapy or contemplative Christianity.

However highly individuated, a culture of awakening can never be a private affair. Such a culture is always an expression of a community. To achieve maturity and depth it requires cultivation over generations. Community is the living link between individuation and social engagement. A culture of awakening simply cannot occur without being rooted in a coherent and vital sense of community, for a matrix of friendships is the very soil in which dharma practice is cultivated. How to create an authentic community, which provides a sound basis for the emergence of a culture while optimizing individual freedom, may be the single most important question facing those practicing the dharma today.

One of the strengths of religious Buddhism is its ability to respond unambiguously to this question through continued establishment of hierarchic institutions that have weathered centuries of turmoil and change. While such institutions may provide excellent settings for sustained training in meditation and reflection, it is questionable whether they alone can provide a sufficient basis for the creation of a contemporary culture of awakening. The democratic and agnostic imperatives of the secular world demand not another Buddhist Church, but an individuated community, where creative imagination and social engagement are valued as highly as philosophic reflection and meditative attainment.

An agnostic Buddhist vision of a culture of awakening will inevitably challenge many of the time-honored roles of religious Buddhism. No longer will it see the role of Buddhism as providing pseudoscientific authority on subjects such as cosmology, biology, and consciousness as it did in prescientific Asian cultures. Nor will it see its role as offering consoling assurances of a better afterlife by living in accord with the worldview of karma and rebirth. Rather than the pessimistic Indian doctrine of temporal degeneration, it will emphasize the freedom and responsibility to create a more awakened and compassionate society on this earth. Instead of authoritarian, monolithic institutions, it could imagine a decentralized tapestry of small-scale, autonomous communities of awakening. Instead of a mystical religious movement ruled by autocratic leaders, it would foresee a deep agnostic, secular culture founded on friendships and governed by collaboration.

# SOURCES AND
# NOTES

The primary sources of this book are those with whom I have studied and trained in dharma practice. In particular, I am indebted to my teachers the late Geshes Ngawang Dargyey and Tamdrin Rabten of Sera Je Monastery, Lhasa, Tibet, and the late Kusan Pangjang Sunim of Songgwang Sa Monastery, near Suncheon, South Korea.

While sources for all quoted passages are given in the notes below, a comprehensive bibliography of writings that have served as an inspiration for this book would be out of place. Two books in particular, however, deserve special mention both as sources for several quoted passages and as introductions to the two main streams of Buddhist thought:

Nanamoli Thera (Osbert Moore). *The Life of the Buddha*. Kandy, Sri Lanka: Buddhist Publishing Society, 1992 (1st edition 1972).

Shantideva. *The Bodhicaryavatara*. (1) Translated from Sanskrit by Kate Crosby and Andrew Skilton. Oxford/New York: Oxford University Press, 1996. (2) Translated from Tibetan by Stephen Batchelor as *A Guide to the Bodhisattva's Way of Life*. Dharamsala, India: Library of Tibetan Works and Archives, 1979.

For background information on Buddhist history as well as sketches of Buddhist figures, schools, and doctrines, the reader might refer to *How the Swans Came to the Lake: A Narrative History of Buddhism in America* by Rick Fields (Boston: Shambhala, 1981), and my *The Awakening of the West: The Encounter of Buddhism and Western Culture* (Berkeley: Parallax, 1994).

## GROUND

*Do not be satisfied with hearsay* . . . is from the *Kalama Sutta* (*Anguttara Nikaya* III: 65), in *The Life of the Buddha*, trans. Nanamoli Thera, 175–76.

### Awakening

*As long as my vision was not fully clear* . . . is from the *Dhammacakkappavatana Sutta* (*Samyutta Nikaya* LVI: 11). A complete translation is found in *The Life of the Buddha*, trans. Nanamoli Thera, 43–45.

This chapter, a reflection on the *Dhammacakkappavatana Sutta,* is indebted to the writings of Nanavira Thera (Harold Musson) collected in *Clearing the Path* (Colombo, Sri Lanka:

Path Press, 1987). The analogy from *Alice's Adventures in Wonderland* and the idea that the four truths are injunctions to act as opposed to propositions to believe are found in *Clearing the Path*, pp. 258–59, while the notion of awakening being "knocked off its pedestal" is found on p. 282. The critique of Buddhism as mysticism is likewise influenced by Nanavira. For a study of the life and work of this remarkable English Buddhist monk and writer, see my "Existence, Enlightenment and Suicide: The Dilemma of Nanavira Thera," in *The Buddhist Forum Volume IV: Seminar Papers 1994–1996*, ed. Tadeusz Skorupski (London: School of Oriental and African Studies), 9–34.

All views attributed in this chapter and elsewhere to "the Buddha" or "Gautama" refer to the Buddha as represented in the Pali Canon.

## Agnosticism

*Suppose, Malunkyaputta, a man . . .* is abridged from the *Culamalunkya Sutta* (*Majjhima Nikaya* 63), in *The Middle Length Discourses of the Buddha*, trans. Nanamoli Thera and Bhikku Bodhi (Boston: Wisdom, 1995), 534–36.

I am indebted to Trevor Ling's *The Buddha: Buddhist Civilization in India and Ceylon* (London: Temple Smith, 1973) for the notion of religion as a "residual civilisation." Rather than stating that Buddhism is a civilization, however, I will argue that Buddhism is akin to a culture.

p. 17 "the rigorous application of a single principle" and all following quotes from T. H. Huxley are from his 1889 essay "Agnosticism," included in *Science and the Christian Tradition* (London: Macmillan, 1904), 245–46. Within less than twenty years Huxley's newly coined term was applied to Buddhism by Ananda Metteyya (Allan Bennett), the second Western European to be ordained as a Buddhist monk. In a letter to the 1904 Free Thought Congress, he wrote: "The position of Buddhism on these vital problems is exactly coincidental, in its fundamental ideas, with the modern agnostic philosophy of the West . . ." See *Buddhism: An Illustrated Review* (Rangoon) 2 (October 1905): 86. The same issue of this journal (edited by Bennett) contains an article "Buddhism an Agnostic Religion," by Professore Alessandro Costa, pp. 79 seq. The current edition of *Encyclopaedia Britannica* likewise describes Buddhism as a religious form of agnosticism.

p. 20 "that complex whole which includes . . ." is from E. B. Tylor, *Primitive Culture* (London: J. Murray, 1871), 1.

## Anguish

*No conditions are permanent* . . . is a paraphrase of the Pali: *sabbe sankhara anicca, sabbe sankhara dukkha, sabbe dhamma anatta* (literally: "all conditions are impermanent; all conditions are *dukkha*, all phenomena are selfless"). *Dukkha* is commonly translated as "suffering." To account for "*all* conditions" being *dukkha*, I use the term "anguish" when referring to *dukkha* as personal experience of the kind of suffering caused by self-centered craving, and "unreliability" or "uncertainty" when referring to *dukkha* as a characteristic of the conditions of life.

For a more detailed analysis of the traditional legend of Siddhartha Gautama, see my *Alone With Others: An Existential Approach to Buddhism* (New York: Grove, 1983), 25–38. Other ideas in this chapter are further developed in *Flight: An Existential Conception of Buddhism,* Wheel Publication no. 316/317 (Kandy, Sri Lanka: Buddhist Publication Society, 1984).

## Death

*Like a dream, whatever I enjoy* . . . is my translation from the Tibetan text of Shantideva's *Bodhicaryavatara* II: 36. Shantideva was an Indian monk who was active in the early part of the eighth century. The *Bodhicaryavatara* is a seminal work on the Buddhist path, widely used in all Tibetan traditions. See above for the two translations currently available in English.

The reflective meditation on death is based on that found in the Tibetan Buddhist traditions. See, for example, sGam.po.pa, *Jewel Ornament of Liberation*, trans. Herbert V. Guenther (London: Rider, 1970), 41–54.

### Rebirth

*But if there is no other world* ... is from the *Kalama Sutta* (*Anguttara Nikaya* III: 65), in *The Life of the Buddha*, trans. Nanamoli Thera, 177.

Some of the arguments in this chapter are further developed in my article "Rebirth: A Case for Buddhist Agnosticism," *Tricycle* 2 (Fall 1992): 16–23. For a study of Buddhist proofs of rebirth, see Martin Willson, *Rebirth and the Western Buddhist* (London: Wisdom, 1987). For accounts of research into cases of those who remember previous lives, see the work of Dr. Ian Stevenson, for example, his *Cases of the Reincarnation Type*, vols. 1–4 (Charlottesville, VA: The University Press of Virginia, 1975–83). For a critique of evidence used to support the theory of life after death, see Susan Blackmore, *Dying to Live: Science and the Near-Death Experience* (London: Grafton, 1993).

p. 37 "Karma is intention. . . ." See, for instance, *Anguttara Nikaya* VI: 13. The psychological function of intention is developed in the chapter "Becoming" below. The Buddha's denial "that karma alone was sufficient to explain the origin of individual experience" is found in the *Sivaka Sutta* (*Samyutta Nikaya: Vedana* 21), where he speaks of eight conditions (the three bodily humors of phlegm, bile, and wind individually and together; seasonal change; improper care; exertion; the ripening of former actions) that lead to feelings of pleasure, pain, etc., only the last of which is karma. The passage is translated in Nanavira Thera, *Clearing the Path*, (Colombo, Sri Lanka: Path Press, 1987), 486–87.

### Resolve

*When crows find a dying snake* . . . is my translation from the Tibetan text of Shantideva's *Bodhicaryavatara* VII: 52.

### Integrity

*A monk asked Yun Men* . . . is the fourteenth case in *The Blue Cliff Record*, 3 vols., trans. Thomas and J. C. Cleary (Boulder/ London: Shambhala, 1977) 1 : 94. *The Blue Cliff Record* is a twelfth-century Chinese collection of koans widely used in Zen Buddhism.

### Friendship

*Just as the dawn* . . . is an anonymous translation of a passage from *Samyutta Nikaya* V.

p. 53 "free and protected space. . . ." I owe this idea to my Jungian analyst Dora Kalff. See Dora M. Kalff, *Sandplay: A Psychotherapeutic Approach to the Psyche* (Los Angeles: Sigo, 1980).

## PATH

*One day an old man was circumambulating* . . . is from *dKa gdams kyi skyes bu dam pa rnams kyi gsung bgros thor bu rnams (Miscellaneous Advice of the Kadampa Masters)*, ed. Tsun ba je gom, Tibetan blockprint, n. d., 41–42. This translation is my own reworking of that made in Geshe Wangyal, *The Door of Liberation* (Boston: Wisdom, 1995), 100. The final reply of Drom differs from both the Tibetan text and Geshe Wangyal's translation; I have substituted a version heard from Tibetan lamas.

## Awareness

*And further, a monk knows . . .* is a rendition of a passage from the *Satipatthana Sutta (Majjhima Nikaya* 10*),* in *The Middle Length Discourses of the Buddha,* trans. Nanamoli Thera and Bhikkhu Bodhi (Boston: Wisdom, 1995), 146.

The practice of mindful awareness meditation described in this chapter is based on the *Satipatthana Sutta* (as above), Shantideva's *Bodhicaryavatara* v, and oral teachings from the contemporary "Insight" (Vipassana) tradition. For an account of insight meditation, see Joseph Goldstein and Jack Kornfield, *Seeking the Heart of Wisdom: The Path of Insight Meditation* (Boston: Shambhala, 1987).

## Becoming

*Confusion conditions activity . . .* is my rendition of the Pali formulation of what are commonly known as the "Twelve Links of Dependent Origination."

The meditation section that begins: "Sit still and come back to the breath" offers a reflection on the five primary constituents of mental life: impact, mood, perception, intention, attention. These are known as the *nama* factors in Theravada Buddhism. In the Pali Canon the Buddha lists them to describe the *nama* (literally "name") dimension of *namarupa* (literally "name-form"), paraphrased here as "embodied personality." In the Tibetan traditions they appear as the five "omnipresent" mental processes as found in Asanga's *Abhidharmasamuccaya.* See Geshe Rabten, *The Mind and Its Functions,* trans. and ed. Stephen Batchelor (Mont Pelerin, Switzerland: Editions Rabten Choeling, 1992), 110–15.

The doctrine of the Twelve Links of Dependent Origination is a key Buddhist teaching, usually explained to describe a process of becoming that occurs over three lifetimes—

although there appears to be no explicit mention of a three-lifetime model in the Buddha's own discourses on the subject in the Pali Canon. An accessible traditional account of the Twelve Links is found in His Holiness the Fourteenth Dalai Lama, *The Meaning of Life from a Buddhist Perspective*, trans. and ed. Jeffrey Hopkins (Boston: Wisdom, 1992).

## Emptiness

*Unborn emptiness has let go of . . .* is my translation of a passage from the fourteenth-century Tibetan lama Tsongkhapa's *rTsa she tik chen rigs pa'i rgya mtso* (Sarnath: 1973), 431. This work is a commentary to Nagarjuna's second-century text *Mulamadhyamakakarika* (*Root Verses on the Center*). The quoted passage forms part of Tsongkhapa's commentary to chapter 24, verse 18, which reads: "Whatever is contingently emergent / Is said to be emptiness. / It is contingently configured, / It is the central path."

This presentation of the doctrine of emptiness is based on the interpretations of Tsongkhapa and his followers in the Geluk school of Tibetan Buddhism. See Geshe Rabten, *Echoes of Voidness*, trans. and ed. Stephen Batchelor (London: Wisdom, 1983), and the introduction to Robert Thurman, *Tsong Khapa's Speech of Gold in the Essence of True Eloquence: Reason and Enlightenment in the Central Philosophy of Tibet* (Princeton: Princeton University Press, 1984).

## Compassion

*Even when I do things . . .* is my translation from the Tibetan text of Shantideva's *Bodhicaryavatara* VIII: 116.

The opening meditation is based on oral Tibetan Buddhist teachings. The discussion of empathy follows Shantideva's *Bodhicaryavatara* VIII: 90 seq. For a Theravada perspective on this subject, see Sharon Salzburg, *Loving Kindness: The Revolutionary Art of Happiness* (Boston: Shambhala, 1995).

# FRUITION

*The way of the Buddha is to know yourself*... is a rendition of Dogen's *Genjo Koan (Actualizing the Fundamental Point)* 4, from his magnum opus, *Shobogenzo*. For a translation of *Genjo Koan*, see *Moon in a Dewdrop: Writings of Zen Master Dogen*, ed. Kazuaki Tanahashi (Berkeley: North Point Press, 1985), 69–73.

## Freedom

*Therefore we know that, unawakened*... is from Philip B. Yampolsky, *The Platform Sutra of the Sixth Patriarch* (New York: Columbia University Press, 1967), 151.

The final three chapters of the book ("Freedom," "Imagination," and "Culture") are inspired by the doctrine of the Three "Bodies" (*trikaya*) of the Buddha: sometimes literally translated as the "Dharma Body" (*dharmakaya*); "Enjoyment Body" (*sambhogakaya*); and "Manifestion Body" (*nirmanakaya*). At the same time the chapters trace the trajectory of the first five stages of the "Noble Eightfold Path" from authentic vision via authentic ideas to authentic speech, action, and livelihood.

The "intrinsic freedom of reality" is a paraphrase of the Mahayana Buddhist doctrine that all phenomena are "intrinsically nirvanic" (Sanskrit: *prakriti-parinirvrita*). It also refers to the idea in the Tibetan practice of Dzogchen of the "self-freeing" nature of phenomena. For Dzogchen, see *The Flight of the Garuda*, trans. Keith Dowman (Boston: Wisdom, 1994).

The themes of perplexity, unknowing, and mystery are

dealt with in my *The Faith to Doubt: Glimpses of Buddhist Uncertainty* (Berkeley: Parallax, 1990).

## Imagination

*[A] a talent for speaking differently* . . . is from Richard Rorty, *Contingency, Irony and Solidarity* (Cambridge: Cambridge University Press, 1989), 7. This book, as well as other non-specialist writings of Rorty, has been a great source of inspiration in the writing of *Buddhism Without Beliefs*. Rorty's style of thinking is particularly helpful in the task of finding a contemporary, nonreligious way of expressing Buddhist ideas. Other books that have had a similar effect are: Milan Kundera, *The Art of the Novel* (New York: Grove, 1986) and *Testaments Betrayed: An Essay in Nine Parts* (London: Faber, 1995), as well as Don Cupitt, *The Time Being* (London: SCM, 1992).

This chapter draws on and develops material first explored in my essay "A Democracy of the Imagination," *Tricycle* 4, no. 2 (Fall 1994): 70–75.

The notion of "self-creation" is a literal rendering of the Tibetan *bdag bskyed*, which traditionally refers to the process of imagining oneself in the form of a "god," a Vajra-yana practice of the *bskyed rim* ("creation stage") in the *Mahanuttara-yoga-tantras*. An overview of such practices is found in *The Jewel in the Lotus: A Guide to the Buddhist Traditions of Tibet*, ed. Stephen Batchelor (London: Wisdom, 1987), 46–57.

## Culture

*There is nothing not practiced* . . . is my translation from the Tibetan text of Shantideva's *Bodhicaryavatara* v: 100.

The notion of individuation is based on the use of the term in the analytical psychology of C. G. Jung. See, for example, Jung's essays: "Conscious, Unconscious, and Individuation," and "A Study in the Process of Individuation," in vol. 9, part 1 of *The Collected Works of C. G. Jung*, trans. R. F. C. Hull (New York/Princeton: Bollingen Foundation, 1968). A seminal work on the concept of Buddhist social engagement is Thich Nhat Hanh, *Being Peace* (Berkeley: Parallax, 1987).

Stephen Batchelor was born in Scotland and educated in Buddhist monasteries in India, Switzerland, and Korea. He has translated and written several books on Buddhism, including *A Guide to the Bodhisattva's Way of Life*, *Alone with Others*, *The Faith to Doubt*, *The Tibet Guide* (winner of the 1988 Thomas Cook Award), and *The Awakening of the West* (joint-winner of the 1994 Tricycle Award). He lectures and conducts meditation retreats worldwide, is a contributing editor of *Tricycle*, and is Director of Studies of the Sharpham College for Buddhist Studies and Contemporary Enquiry, Devon, England.